The
Creative
Hostess
YORK
&
HARROGATE
COOKBOOK

We would like to thank all those who have helped us in the preparation of this book, particularly:
Hilary McGowan MA, Deputy Curator, The Castle Museum and all the restaurateurs and chefs listed on pages 78-79 who have so kindly provided us with recipes.

THE CHAINED RED PRINTER'S DEVIL

This little fiend can be seen in Coffee Yard, Stonegate, over the doorway of the oldest printing shop in York. It is the old trade sign of printers, and earned apprentices to the craft the nickname of "printers' devils". We dedicate this drawing to their present day colleagues — devils and angels alike — without whom this little volume would not exist!

FIREMARKS *(see previous page)* in the York Castle Museum date from Georgian times — before the days of the municipal brigade — and are still to be seen on some shops and houses in York. Insurance companies ran their own fire engines and would only come to the aid of customers in the case of fire if the appropriate company plaque was displayed.

First published 1984 by
Marion Edwards Limited,
69 Abingdon Road,
Kensington W8 6AW

ISBN 0 904330 64 8
Printed in England by
T.J. Press (Padstow) Ltd.
Cornwall

The Creative Hostess
YORK
&
HARROGATE
COOKBOOK

ILLUSTRATED
BY
GERALDINE
MARCHAND

Introduction

This volume is one of a series devised to entertain and enlighten cooks and travellers alike. It offers the reader a selection of recipes for dishes popular with visitors to some of York's and Harrogate's leading restaurants and hotels, combining these with delightful drawings and fascinating facts about the towns and their history. It is difficult to choose between the quite different but complementary attractions of Harrogate and York. Harrogate combines the elegance of a spa town with all the facilities of a modern conference centre, whilst York's medieval splendours are a joy to behold. It is lucky for the visitor that they are so close to one another.

Yorkshire can claim more than its fair share of individualists. Many of the characters who step larger than life from the pages of our history books are sons and daughters of this famous county — men like Captain Cook the explorer, Dick Turpin the highwayman (born in Essex, but widely accepted as 'belonging' to York), the unfortunate Guy Fawkes (whose demise all English children gleefully celebrate every fifth of November), and women like Amy Johnson the aviator, and those talented nineteenth century novelists the Brontë sisters. Many twentieth century personalities famous for their character and outspokenness also hail from Yorkshire — the extraordinary Sitwell family, sportsmen Harvey Smith and Geoffrey Boycott, and former Prime Minister Sir Harold Wilson, to name but a few.

We found this individuality to be reflected in the food served in York and Harrogate today. Whilst Roast Beef and Yorkshire Pudding will surely never lose their popularity, they now take their place on menus alongside a variety of culinary delights with far-flung origins. It is perhaps in the teatime category that traditional favourites still have the firmest hold with Parkin and Yorkshire Curd Tart amongst the most popular. (Was Michael Parkinson's great-grandfather a baker, we wonder?)

There are a million good reasons for spending time in Yorkshire, so whether you are a tourist in York, a conference participant in Harrogate, or are lucky enough to live locally, enjoy with us the delightful combination of culinary, architectural and historical pleasures which these very distinctive towns have to offer.

A note on measures and conversions
Ingredients are given in metric, Imperial and American measures. **Use measures from one column only.** Teaspoon and tablespoon measures in the metric column correspond to 5 ml and 15 ml respectively. Unless otherwise stated, all fruits and vegetables used in these recipes should be medium-sized.

Contents

THE CHAPTER HOUSE, YORK MINSTER

'Eborakon' meaning 'place where yew trees grow' was the name given by the ancient Britons to the place of worship which has now become the City of York. Eboracum, as the Romans called it, grew from a military outpost to become the capital of Roman Britain in the North. Offering a variety of shops and booths, a temple and a huge public baths, it was a bustling, cosmopolitan centre. Situated on the river Foss, it was also the scene of extensive trading in goods such as pottery, corn, jewellery and lead.

The Anglo Saxons used the name 'Eoforwic', later changed by the Vikings to Jorvik and finally emerging as York.

Lasting impressions

410 A.D. marked the end of the Roman era, and although the City's importance dwindled, the former inhabitants left a permanent reminder of their presence — the legionary fortress is still at the centre of the City and today's traffic hums along the old Roman roads and routes. Stand on almost any street corner in York and you will also see reminders of the Danish occupation — Peasgate, Skeldergate, Goodramgate and Petergate — 'gate' being Old Norse for street.

The following phase in the City's history was something of a step backwards. Full of confidence after his victory at the Battle of Hastings, William the Conqueror marched into York, destroying records and demolishing buildings to make room for the construction of two castles. Not the most popular visitor to York, he did his best to punish and subdue the townsfolk who strongly objected to the Norman presence.

Fluctuating fortunes

Undeterred by the devastation inflicted by William, the citizens of medieval York revived the town's importance and prosperity, helped by the fact that the City was a key military point and a natural market centre. Fine medieval buildings still line many of the streets in York, reminding us of the affluence of that period. The City also enjoyed a religious boom — it had great ecclesiastical status and was the proud possessor of fifty parish churches and two large abbeys as well as the Minster! Not always a pleasant place to visit, York was referred to by Edward III as one of the most disgusting places in his kingdom! He was probably quite justified in his opinion as every gutter held rotting offal thrown out by butchers, and the town's privies were positioned on the Ouse Bridge and around the moat. Attempts were made at sweetening the City's atmosphere. The Shambles, which was the butcher's street, was particularly bad, but a sixteenth century order which declared that all pigsties should be destroyed met with little success!

The Dissolution brought a swift end to York's monasteries and many of its religious establishments. Public protest failed to make any impression, as Roger Aske discovered when he organised the Pilgrimage of Grace and was punished by being hung in chains from Clifford's Tower until he was dead. The Civil War brought further instability when the staunchly Royalist City of York was beseiged. The defeat of the Royalists by the Parliamentarians at the Battle of Marston effectively ended all further resistance.

An elegant era

In the eighteenth century, York became *the* place to be seen — a northern equivalent to London or Bath. It was an elegant age in which dancing and card-playing took priority in the fashionable Assembly Rooms, which formed the hub of the town's social activity. An abundance of coffee houses sprang up, along with a theatre and a bowling green. Visitors enjoyed the fast-growing sport of horse racing and a constant stream of

Continued on page 10 . . .

YORK MINSTER *The first Minster stood on this site as long ago as 627 A.D. You can read more about it on page 46.*

ST. WILLIAM'S COLLEGE, YORK

This splendid medieval college is one of the best preserved timber buildings in England. It was founded in 1461 by Warwick the King Maker as a college to house Chantry priests, whose official occupation was saying mass for the dead. However, it appears from our researches that many of the younger members also pursued other, less religious activities!

10

Continued from page 7 . . .
fairs and shows kept the townsfolk entertained. Striving to cater for all tastes, even a licensed brothel was provided!

Hang around!

While today's visitors are drawn by the wealth of history and picturesque sights, nineteenth century folk came to York for different reasons. Travelling on special excursion trains, they flocked from near and far to enjoy hangings outside the City's courtrooms. Given a good programme, this popular event sometimes drew a crowd of ten thousand, with street entertainers, pedlars and thimble-riggers* creating a carnival atmosphere.

These forerunners of today's three card tricksters used a pea under three cups or walnut shells to part unsuspecting visitors from the contents of their purses.

BOOTSCRAPERS *are still to be found by the doorways of shops and houses in York. They are a relic from the days when the City was not cobbled throughout and was consequently a rather muddy place!*

Sweets for the sweet

Some latterday associations are of a more palatable nature — everyone with a sweet tooth should know that York is the home of some of Britain's leading chocolate bars! Mary Tuke, a Quaker, opened a grocery shop in 1725, which was eventually inherited by Henry Rowntree. You can read more about his family on page 63.

York is also the birthplace of Terry's chocolate. Originally an eighteenth century confectionery shop making Pontefract cakes, acid drops and gumballs, by 1886 Terry's had grown into a thriving chocolate factory.

York today

Several million people now come to York every year. The City which was once described as having 'great corruptions and horrible pernicious air', is today a delight to visit.

BETTY'S BAR *Evidence of the City's more recent history is to be found in Betty's Bar in Davygate. This used to be a favourite haunt of World War II pilots, and many of them carved their initials in a mirror frame which is still to be seen there.*

(Footnote!)

"Now, good digestion wait on appetite, and health on both!"
Macbeth
WILLIAM SHAKESPEARE, 1564-1616

DEEP FRIED MUSHROOMS WITH CUCUMBER MAYONNAISE

Serves 2

Here's how Harrogate's Hospitality Inn serve their golden brown mushrooms in a sumptuous dressing. An excellent way to start off a meal!

Metric		lb/oz	U.S.A.
275 g	*Mushrooms, whole*	10 oz	2 cups
3 tbsp	*Mayonnaise*	3 tbsp	¼ cup
¼	*Cucumber, diced*	¼	¼ cup
150 ml	*Milk*	¼ pt	½ cup
1	*Egg, beaten*	1	1
125 g	*Flour, seasoned*	4 oz	1 cup
175 g	*Fresh breadcrumbs*	6 oz	3 cups
	Oil for deep frying		
3	*Lettuce leaves, shredded*	3	3

1. Mix the mayonnaise and cucumber and refrigerate for an hour to chill.
2. Mix the milk and egg and season with salt and pepper.
3. De-stalk the mushrooms* then wash and dry in a clean cloth. Coat the mushrooms in the flour, dip into the egg and milk mixture and finally coat with the breadcrumbs.
4. Place the oil in a deep fryer or chip pan and heat to 170°C, 325°F. Put the mushrooms in a frying basket and lower into the hot fat for about 1 minute until golden brown.
5. Spread the lettuce on two plates and arrange the mushrooms on top. Serve the cucumber mayonnaise separately.

* The stalks may be used in soup or salad — Editor.

THE SHAMBLES, YORK

This charming street is said to be a thousand years old and is certainly the only York street to be mentioned in the Domesday Book. With its overhanging buildings, old casements and blackened beams, it epitomizes our romantic expectations of a 'medieval street'. There was, however, a time when it must have been singularly unsavoury. Not only was it a centre for butchers in the days before refrigeration and proper waste disposal, but refuse was just thrown into the gutters.

The Shambles takes its name either from the Anglo-Saxon 'shamel' meaning a stall or bench on which meat was displayed, or it may come from the old English word for a slaughter house. Whatever its derivations, we have no hesitation in recommending an amble along the Shambles!

AVOCADO MEDITERRANO   *Serves 8*

At Ristorante Bari in the Shambles, the Italian chefs, Angelo, Mario, and Franco serve this tasty seafood treat.

Metric		*lb/oz*	*U.S.A.*
	4 Avocados, soft		
1	*Lemon, juice of*	1	1
1 tbsp	*Oil*	1 tbsp	1 tbsp
1	*Onion, chopped*	1	1
1	*Red pepper*	1	1
225 g	*Seafood, cooked**	8 oz	8 oz
125 g	*Mozzarella cheese*	4 oz	¼ lb

* *Use a selection as available, which could include prawns, mussels, cockles and squid.*

1. Cut the avocados in half, remove the stones and rub the flesh with lemon juice to prevent discoloration.
2. Heat the oil and gently fry the onions until tender but not browned. De-seed the pepper and cut into fine slivers. Add to the onion and cook for a few more minutes.
3. Stir in the seafood and cook over a gentle heat until all are heated through.
4. Spoon on to the avocado pears and top with thinly sliced cheese.
5. Place under a hot grill for a few minutes until the cheese has melted and nicely browned.

WHIP-MA-WHOP-MA-GATE *is to be found where The Shambles meets The Pavement. It is named after a form of rough justice for felons: they were tied to the back of a cart which was then pulled through the streets allowing anyone to take a swipe at the unfortunate victim. Traditionally his ordeal ended at Whip-ma-whop-ma-gate.*

THEATRE ROYAL SALADS

York's Theatre Royal Restaurant offers, among others, two tangy salads based on cucumber. Mix together bite-sized chunks of cucumber and fresh grapefruit segments, adding a little of the grated rind and pouring over any juice. Chill before serving. Alternatively, mix the cucumber with chopped pineapple. For a sweeter salad, make these with tinned fruit. These recipes come from Susan Swindell and Joanna Garbutt, as does that for the salad below.

CURRIED RICE SALAD   Serves 6-8

Metric		lb/oz	U.S.A.
225 g	Long grain rice	8 oz	1 cup
60 g	Sultanas	2 oz	⅓ cup
60 g	Peanuts	2 oz	⅓ cup
2 tbsp	Curry powder*	2 tbsp	2 tbsp

* Mix with a little oil or vinaigrette if preferred — Editor.

1. Cook the rice in 4 cups of boiling, salted water for 12–15 minutes.
2. When the rice is tender, pour into a colander and rinse under the cold water tap. Drain well.
3. When the rice is cold and quite dry, turn into a bowl.
4. Add the remaining ingredients and mix together until all the rice is the orange brown colour of the curry powder.
5. Turn into a clean bowl and serve.

* Mix with a little oil or vinaigrette if preferred — Editor.

HOT CREAMED MORECAMBE SHRIMPS   Serves 4

This shrimp delicacy is an imaginative (and extremely delicious) version of traditional seaside fare, from the Number 6 Restaurant in Harrogate.

Metric		lb/oz	U.S.A.
	6 × 50 g (1¾ oz) Potted shrimps		
200 ml	Double cream	⅓ pt	¾ cup
½ tsp	Anchovy essence	½ tsp	½ tsp
½ tsp	Paprika	½ tsp	½ tsp

1. Put the potted shrimps, cream and anchovy essence into a small pan.
2. Place over a low heat, stirring all the time.
3. Increase the heat and cook for 5–10 minutes, stirring continuously till the liquid is reduced and the cream starts to thicken.
4. Spoon into serving dishes and sprinkle with the paprika. Serve with hot toast.

THE LITTLE ADMIRAL, *resplendent in his blue and white uniform, can be seen standing over the clock outside St. Martin's in Coney Street, York. Glance up to check the time and you will see this unexpected figure.*

TROUT SNUGGLES   *Serves 4*

These light pastry savouries, with their delicious trout and spinach toppings, are served coated in Noilly cream sauce or Port and mushroom cream sauce (recipes on page 76) in Hodgson's Restaurant at the Russell Hotel, Harrogate.

Metric		lb/oz	U.S.A.
	1 × 275 g (10 oz) Fresh trout		
1 tsp	*Butter*	1 tsp	1 tsp
125 g	*Button mushrooms, sliced*	4 oz	1 cup
1	*Nutmeg, pinch of*	1	1
3 tbsp	*Double cream*	3 tbsp	¼ cup
4	*Large spinach leaves*	4	4
125 g	*Puff pastry*	4 oz	4 oz
1	*Egg, beaten*	1	1

1. Set the oven to 220°C, 425°F, Gas Mark 7.
2. Fillet the trout then remove the skin,cutting each fillet into two. Season with salt and pepper.
3. Melt the butter in a pan and cook the mushrooms with the nutmeg. Season with salt and pepper. Stir in the cream and bring to the boil. Reduce the heat, simmer for one minute, then leave to cool.
4. Dip the spinach leaves into boiling water for a minute to just blanch them. Remove and place in cold water, then drain well.
5. Roll out the pastry and cut into four rectangles about 9 × 5 cm (3½" × 2").
6. Season the trout with salt and black pepper and roll up a half fillet on each spinach leaf, making a neat 'parcel'.
7. Spoon the mushroom mixture on to the pastry rectangles, and place a 'parcel' on top. Brush the edges with egg then bake for 20–25 minutes until golden brown.

ST. MICHAEL'S, SPURRIERGATE *A curfew is tolled here every night at eight o'clock. The custom began when a benefactor, lost in the forest of Galtres, managed to find his way back to safety, guided by the sound of York's bells.*

YORK CASTLE MUSEUM

John Kirk was a North Yorkshire medical practitioner who should be regarded as the patron saint of hoarders! He had a habit of collecting all sorts of Victorian everyday objects, seeming to realise that the bits and pieces which people at the time regarded as little more than rubbish, would fascinate future generations.

The City of York converted the eighteenth century Female and Debtors' Prisons into a museum to house Kirk's collection. It has proved a great success, vividly recreating scenes from the past and still intriguing today's visitors with items such as an early electric heater which bears the instruction to first time users — 'How to light an electric fire — switch it on'!

THE EYE OF YORK is an area around which are three imposing buildings: the Female and Debtors' Prisons (which have now been converted into the Castle Museum), and the Assize Courts. In former days the 'eye' of the law could fairly be said to be upon you if you found yourself having dealings with any one of these institutions!

J BELL
TOBACCO AND SNUFF
MRS AND DEALER

THE GILDED HORSE'S HEAD *outside 76 Petergate, York dates from the time when the premises was a tobacconist's shop. Although very attractive, it was not merely decorative — in former days it spurted a gas flame from its mouth for smokers wanting a light!*

CALAMARES EN SU TINTA   *Serves 4-6*

Emilio Rivera of Emilio's Restaurant, Harrogate has provided us with this culinary delight. Though it entails a fair amount of preparation, take it from us, it's worth it!

Metric		lb/oz	U.S.A.
	700–900 g (1½–2 lb) Squid		
3 tbsp	*Olive oil*	3 tbsp	¼ cup
2	*Garlic cloves, crushed*	2	2
2	*Onions, chopped*	2	1 cup
125 ml	*Dry white wine*	4 fl. oz	½ cup
1	*Small chilli*	1	1
	Chicken stock or water*		
15 g	*Breadcrumbs*	½ oz	¼ cup
4 tbsp	*Chopped parsley*	4 tbsp	⅓ cup

Although squid is not often seen in fish shops the use of fresh squid is recommended, and your local fishmonger should be able to acquire it for you. Small fish 250–275 g (8–10 oz) will be the best quality. Ask your fishmonger to remove the backbone and stomach, reserving the small inkbag located in the stomach.

1. Wash the squid well and then chop the tentacles and body into small pieces 2.5 cm (1") long.
2. Place the oil in a pan with the garlic and heat gently for 3-4 minutes. Remove the garlic and add the onion and squid. Fry gently for 10–15 minutes.
3. Put the inkbags and wine in a liquidizer and blend for a few seconds. Strain on to the squid and add the chilli. Cook over a low heat until the squid is tender, adding a little stock or water* if the juice has dried up. Season with salt and pepper, and remove the chilli. Stir in the breadcrumbs.
4. Divide the mixture between small serving dishes and sprinkle with parsley.

HANSOM CABS *took their name from Joseph Hansom, their inventor, a York man who was born in Micklegate in 1803.*

Harrogate could be said to owe its prosperity to a small bird known locally as a tewit, but more generally referred to by ornithologists as a peewit. In 1571 a certain Captain William Slingsby of Bilton is said to have been riding by the two small hamlets which then made up Harrogate when his attention was arrested by a flock of tewits. Having stopped to watch the birds, Captain Slingsby noticed a spring in the ground. He was familiar with the continental health resorts, and recognised it to be a mineral spring.

The Tewit well

This was the beginning of Harrogate's growth into a famous spa town. Slingsby had the immediate area around the spring paved and walled and it became known as the Tewit Well after the birds that helped lead to its discovery.

After Captain Slingsby's discovery many more springs were found and there are 89 recorded in and around Harrogate. They exist because a tremendous disturbance in the earth's crust thousands of years ago folded and twisted the different layers of rock so pocketing the waters and bringing them to the surface.

A fashionable spa

Harrogate reached its heyday as a fashionable spa in the nineteenth century. Its geographical position helped boost its popularity — only 20 miles from York, it is equidistant from east and west coasts, and approximately 200 miles from both Edinburgh and London. In all ways it was ideally situated in the very heart of England, en route to and from just about everywhere.

The medicinal qualities of the waters had long been known but suddenly they were no longer merely good for you but fashionable as well! Thus, along with all the genuine patients with their real medical ailments came the gentry and the idle nobility bringing with them their

Continued overleaf

THE ROYAL BATHS, HARROGATE

Reputed to have been the finest in Europe when they were opened in 1897, the Royal Baths in Harrogate are still very up-to-date. Treatments offered include Turkish baths, saunas, a solarium and a small fresh water swimming pool.

The Royal Baths were also designed as a fashionable place to meet and be seen. Today the rooms are used by a variety of societies and organisations.

entire households and all their expectations of fine living. Shops, hotels, stylish houses and other elegant buildings sprang up and the town enjoyed enormous prosperity. The custom was to go and drink the waters before breakfast and then to go out around the town: on excursions, shopping, playing cards, visiting the theatre, and so on. Quite a holiday!

Cures at a price!

Although the waters were held to be beneficial, they were actually rather unpleasant since sulphur water smells repugnant. It may be that the very unpleasantness of the waters seemed to guarantee their effectiveness — after all, we don't expect medicine to taste nice! In 1697 Celia Fiennes visited the springs and said of the water, 'it makes a good sort of purge if you can hold your breath long enough as to drink them down'. Evidently her horse thought differently and refused to go near the waters because of the stench.

However, the prevailing medical opinion was definitely that the waters were good for you. A York physician, Edmund Deane, wrote a best-selling book in the 17th century. The waters, he said, 'cheereth and reviveth the spirits, strengtheneth the stomacke, causeth a good and quick appetite'. In 1656 Dr. George Neale of Leeds recommended drinking three to four pints a day. This would undoubtedly have had a drastic purging effect! By the nineteenth century people were also bathing in the waters to relieve skin diseases and other ailments: the Royal Baths offered hot sulphur baths, massage-douche, berthe vapours, liver pack with needle or shower, or the Harrogate carbonic acid bath.

Harrogate's spring waters were certainly good business for everyone concerned, from the first resident physician, employed by the Swan Hydro (a hydropathic company), down to the Queen of Harrogate — one Betty Lupton. Betty ladled out free cups of the foul smelling sulphur water for over 56 years! The waters were even a successful mail order product — an achievement for both the entrepreneur and the post office since they were successfully despatched in glass bottles to a variety of far flung destinations.

RUNSWICK BAY *Once believed to be inhabited by fairies or bogles, this stretch of the coast was the home of Hob Thrush. An amiable 'bogle', he had a great reputation for curing whooping cough so that in his day Runswick enjoyed a 'season' all year round!*

THE STRAY AND MONTPELIER STREET, HARROGATE

The Stray is a vast area of open grassland enjoyed by Harrogate's residents and visitors alike for walks, games, even exercising horses. It is particularly beautiful in spring when great clusters of crocuses appear. Originally pastureland for sheep and cattle, the area was protected in perpetuity against any future development by the Enclosures Act of 1770.

A word to the brave

Adventurous present-day visitors can still try the waters from a sulphur spring in the Royal Pump Room — but we recommend that the faint-hearted hold their breath lest the strong smell overpowers them! If you manage to gulp it down you can rest assured it will be doing you good!

Famous visitors

Daniel Defoe spent time in Harrogate, and **Alfred, Lord Tennyson** came to the spa while he was poet Laureate. **Charles Dickens** remarked after a visit that it was 'the queerest place with the strangest people, leading the oddest lives'!

Even royalty came to take the waters. In 1911 three queens visited it in one day — **Queen Alexandra, the Empress Marie of Russia and Queen Amelie of Portugal**.

In 1926, **Agatha Christie** was 'discovered' in Harrogate after mysteriously disappearing (see page 29).

THE HARROGATE MOUNTIES: *The Stray is so extensive that Harrogate has its own 'Mounties' — policemen on horseback — to patrol it.*

*"Let us have wine and women, mirth and laughter,
Sermons and soda-water the day after."*

Don Juan
GEORGE GORDON, LORD BYRON, 1788-1824

ROAST BEEF

Sirloin is the best joint for roasting, and can be cooked at a high temperature. If using a less tender cut, a lower temperature is preferable. Joints on the bone take 5 minutes less per 450 g (1 lb) to cook than boned and rolled cuts.

Cook boned and rolled Sirloin at 210°C, 425°F, Gas Mark 7 for 25 minutes per 450 g (1 lb) plus 25 minutes. Cook a cheaper boned and rolled cut at 190°C, 375°F, Gas Mark 5 for 33 minutes per 450 g (1 lb) plus 33 minutes.

To make gravy:
1. Pour off the fat from the meat juices discarding most of it but reserving 30 ml, (2 tbsp) in a saucepan.
2. Blend 15 g (1 tbsp) flour into the fat and cook over a gentle heat until it turns brown.
3. Combine the meat juices left in the roasting tin with enough hot stock to make 300 ml (½ pt) of liquid and stir this into the brown roux. Stirring continuously, boil for 2-3 minutes then season, strain and serve.

AN EXOTIC VASE OF FLOWERS in Harrogate Royal Baths is a reminder of the town's connections with horticulture, which began as early as 1843 when the town held its first annual Flower Show. This first show was quite an undertaking since it included balls, musical concerts, puppet shows and boating.

YORKSHIRE PUDDING
Serves 6

The book could not possibly have been complete without the most traditional of traditional Yorkshire greats! Here's how the Micklegate Restaurant at the Ladbroke Abbey Park Hotel, York like to serve their version.

Metric		lb/oz	U.S.A.
600 ml	Milk	1 pt	2½ cups
3	Eggs, beaten	3	3
450 g	Plain flour, sieved	1 lb	4 cups
30 g	Dripping or lard	1 oz	2 tbsp

1. While your beef is cooking make the Yorkshire pudding. Put the milk and eggs into a bowl and beat together with a pinch of salt. Fold in the flour then beat well until you have a smooth batter with plenty of air in the mixture. Leave to stand in a cold place.
2. Thirty minutes before the meat is ready, turn the oven up to 230°C, 450°F, Gas Mark 8 and move the beef down to the middle shelf. Put the fat in the pudding tin and place in the oven until the fat is smoking. Pour in the batter and cook for 15 minutes at the top of the oven until the pudding has fully risen but is still pale in colour.
3. Turn down the heat to 150°C, 300°F, Gas Mark 2 and cook for a further 10 minutes until the pudding is golden brown. Serve at once.

In Yorkshire, the Pudding is still often served as a separate course, with gravy, prior to the meat. This dates from the days when it was necessary to fill up with pudding as a little meat had to go a long way. This recipe produces a very filling pudding. For a lighter version, use half the quantity of flour and 1 egg — Editor.

THE ROYAL PUMP ROOMS, HARROGATE

Those with an interest in economics might like to know that the Royal Pump Rooms were built in 1842 at a cost of only £2,249.0s.7d!

They were built to house the therapeutic sulphur well — known locally as the 'stinking spawr' because of its characteristic smell of bad eggs! It can still be seen — and smelt — in the basement, although the Pump Rooms are now a museum.

The Harrogate headache *became well known. When hydrogen dissolved in the sulphur waters it produced a gas which in small amounts over a long period could lead to a headache (and in large amounts, would be poisonous!) Before the phenomenon was properly understood, local people referred to it as the Harrogate headache. However, the smell is so repulsive it is unlikely that anyone could have stood it long enough to suffer ill effects!*

Harrogate air *is undoubtedly invigorating. Whatever your confidence in the powers of the Harrogate waters, there is no doubt that the bracing fresh air in and around the town is just as likely to bring colour to your cheeks! It was once possible to hire chairs and horse-drawn traps in which to enjoy the air.*

FILLETTO CASANOVA

Serves 4

A Ristorante Bari dish, ideal for a romantic candlelit dinner.

Metric		lb/oz	U.S.A.
	4 Fillet steaks		
2 tbsp	*Olive oil*	2 tbsp	2 tbsp
30 g	*Butter*	1 oz	2 tbsp
125 g	*Pâté*	4 oz	½ cup
125 ml	*Marsala*	4 fl. oz	½ cup
85 ml	*Brandy*	3 fl. oz	⅓ cup

1. Season the steaks with salt and freshly ground black pepper. Rub with a little of the oil and leave to marinate.
2. Heat the remaining oil in a pan until very hot and fry the steaks for a minute on each side or until brown. Remove from the pan and keep warm.
3. Melt the butter and cook the pâté until it turns into a purée, add the Marsala and stir well.
4. Place the steaks in the sauce and heat gently.
5. Put the brandy in a small pan and heat through. Pour over the steaks and flambé. Shake the pan so the brandy burns as long as possible when the meat should be done.

STEAK AND KIDNEY PUDDING   *Serves 4*

A satisfying dish from York's Theatre Royal Restaurant.

Metric		lb/oz	U.S.A.
	450 g (1 lb) Shin beef, trimmed and cubed		
125 g	*Ox kidney, chopped*	4 oz	4 oz
2 tbsp	*Seasoned flour*	2 tbsp	2 tbsp
1 tsp	*Mixed herbs*	1 tsp	1 tsp
2 tsp	*Worcestershire sauce*	2 tsp	2 tsp
2 tbsp	*Sherry*	2 tbsp	2 tbsp
	For the pastry:		
225 g	*Self-raising flour**	8 oz	2 cups
125 g	*Shredded beef suet*	4 oz	1 cup

1. Sift the flour into a mixing bowl with 1 tsp salt and stir in the suet. Mix with a little water to form a smooth dough that leaves the sides of the mixing bowl clean.
2. Turn out on to a floured board. Roll into a round large enough to line the inside of a 1 litre (1½ pt) pudding basin. Cut out a quarter of the round and leave on one side to make the lid. Grease the basin and lift the pastry in carefully. Ease the cut edges together and press to fit the shape of the bowl.
3. To make the filling, toss the steak and kidney in the seasoned flour. Mix in the herbs and Worcestershire sauce.
4. Place the filling in the pudding basin and pour over enough water to come half way up the sides. Add the sherry.
5. Shape the reserved quarter of pastry into a lid and place on top of the pudding, sealing the edges well with water. Cover the top with greased greaseproof paper or foil pleated in the centre. Tie a string handle around the rim to help remove the basin from the hot steamer.
6. Place the basin in a steamer on a pan of gently bubbling water and steam for at least three hours, topping up the water level from time to time during cooking.
7. When cooked, remove the pudding from the steamer. Remove the paper or foil and serve straight from the basin, wrapped in a napkin, with potatoes and vegetables.

* *Add 2 level tsp baking powder to plain flour.*

FOOD FIT FOR HEROES! *This old English dish would undoubtedly have been served to Sebastian in his nursery at Brideshead! Castle Howard, close to both York and Harrogate, has been the magnificent home of the Howard family since the early 18th century, but is probably better known to millions of viewers on both sides of the Atlantic as the mansion featured in the television version of Evelyn Waugh's 'Brideshead Revisited'.*

PAUPIETTES DE BOEUF   *Serves 4*

This French dish is a popular choice at York's Viking Hotel.

Metric		lb/oz	U.S.A.
	450 g (1 lb) Lean beef topside		
125 g	*Veal, minced*	4 oz	½ cup
125 g	*Onion-mustard**	4 oz	½ cup
50 g	*Flour*	2 oz	½ cup
3 tbsp	*Tomato purée*	3 tbsp	¼ cup
3 tbsp	*Dripping*	3 tbsp	¼ cup
125 g	*Carrots, diced*	4 oz	1 cup
2	*Onions, diced*	2	2
900 ml	*Stock*	1½ pt	3½ cups
1	*Bouquet garni*	1	1
125 ml	*Red wine*	¼ pt	½ cup

1. Set the oven to 170°C, 325°F, Gas Mark 3.
2. To make the stuffing, put the veal and two-thirds of the onion-mustard in a bowl with half the flour and 1 tbsp tomato purée. Mix together well.
3. Cut the meat into four slices across the grain. Flatten each slice with a meat mallet then trim each piece to 10 × 8 cm (4" × 3"). Chop trimmings well and add to the stuffing.
4. Season each slice of meat with salt and pepper and remaining onion-mustard. Spread stuffing down the centre of each slice. Roll up neatly and secure with string.
5. Melt the dripping in a pan and fry the paupiettes over a high heat until light brown, to seal the juices. Remove the meat and place in a covered ovenproof dish.
6. Add the vegetables to the pan and cook gently until tender. Remove the vegetables and place in the dish with the meat. Drain off any excess fat from the pan, stir in the remaining flour and cook to a brown roux. Add the remaining tomato purée and stir well. Cool.
7. Bring the stock to the boil and pour into the pan. Bring back to the boil, skim, season, then pour over the meat and vegetables. Add the bouquet garni. Cover and cook in the oven for 1½–2 hours until tender. Transfer to a warm dish, removing strings.
8. Remove the bouquet garni and any fat from the sauce, add the wine and check seasoning. Pour a little over the meat and serve the rest separately.

* Chop half an onion finely, and mix with 85 g (3 oz, ¼ cup) French mustard.

THIS FRENCH DISH *is hardly out of place in Harrogate! In 1946 an enterprising publicity manager came up with the bright idea of 'twinning' Harrogate with a French spa—and Harrogate and Luchon in the Pyrenees were the first towns to twin in this way.*

BISTECCA ALLA PIZZAIOLA   *Serves 4*

From the Ristorante Bar in the Shambles, an easy-to-prepare,
mouthwatering creation of steaks in tomato, garlic and herb
sauce.

Metric		*lb/oz*	*U.S.A.*
	4 × 225 g (8 oz) Sirloin steaks		
2 tbsp	*Oil*	2 tbsp	2 tbsp
900 g	*Tomatoes, skinned, de-seeded and chopped*	2 lb	2 lb
3-4	*Garlic cloves, crushed*	3-4	3-4
1	*Oregano, pinch of*	1	1
2-3	*Capers*	2-3	2-3

1. Pound the steaks well with a rolling pin then season with
   salt and freshly ground black pepper.
2. Melt the oil in a large pan and brown the steaks on both
   sides.
3. In a separate pan, cook the tomatoes with the garlic,
   oregano, capers and salt and pepper until tender.
4. Spread the tomato sauce over the steaks, cover the pan
   with a lid and cook for about 5 minutes.
5. Serve with the sauce.

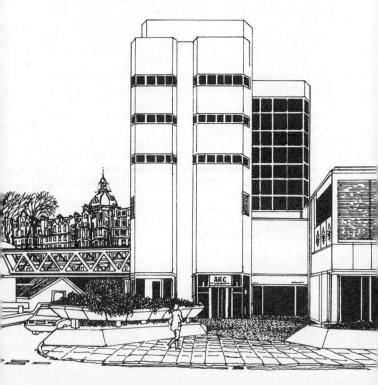

A TOWN OF CONTRASTS

Harrogate not only manages to combine its old and new features successfully — the picture on the left shows the magnificent new Conference Centre with the Majestic Hotel in the background — but also offers the visitor variety and surprises. If you are fascinated by the Orient, don't miss a visit to Mrs. Christie's antique shop. Although she is no relation of the famous writer referred to below, her shop contains many mysteries for the uninitiated.

AGATHA CHRISTIE *disappeared in 1926 much to the consternation of her family and friends, and to the delight of the Press who made it front page news. After some time she was recognised walking in the Swan Hydro gardens where she had gone to ground, one presumes, for peace and quiet.*
More recently film makers, inspired by the mystery still surrounding the episode, came to Harrogate to recreate the 1920's for a film with an imaginative explanation of Agatha Christie's adventure!

RACK OF ENGLISH LAMB
WITH HONEY AND MINT   *Serves 2*

This succulent lamb and honey splendour is just one of a wonderful selection from the Oliver Twist Refectory. Find it in the Hospitality Inn, Harrogate.

Metric		*lb/oz*	*U.S.A.*
	450-500 g (16-18 oz) Best end neck of lamb*		
1 tbsp	*Oil*	1 tbsp	1 tbsp
60 g	*Butter*	2 oz	¼ cup
125 g	*Mushrooms*	4 oz	1 cup
1 tbsp	*Honey*	1 tbsp	1 tbsp
2 tsp	*Mint, chopped*	2 tsp	2 tsp
	Watercress to garnish		

* *Ask your butcher to chine and trim the rack of lamb for you.*

1. Set the oven to 180°C, 350°F, Gas Mark 4. Make a zig-zag pattern with a sharp knife on the white fat, but do not pierce the flesh too deeply. Season with salt and pepper.
2. Heat the oil in a roasting tin then fry the lamb on both sides for 1 minute to seal the juices. Bake for 35 minutes.
3. Melt the butter in a pan and fry the mushrooms gently. Remove and keep warm. Mix the honey and mint together.
4. Five minutes before the lamb is cooked, take out of the oven and strain off the juices. Spread with honey glaze.
5. Return to the oven to glaze. When cooked, transfer to a warm serving dish and pour over any remaining glaze.
6. Decorate with the mushrooms and watercress. Place cutlet frills on the end of the bones.

LEG OF LAMB COOKED IN PASTRY   *Serves 6*

Most of the dishes from Harrogate's Hotel Majestic are fit to serve before the Queen! This unusual dish is no exception.

Metric		*lb/oz*	*U.S.A.*
	1 Leg of lamb, boned*		
60 g	*Butter*	2 oz	¼ cup
60 g	*Carrots, diced*	2 oz	½ cup
1	*Onion, chopped*	1	1
½	*Garlic clove*	½	½
30 g	*Fresh breadcrumbs*	1 oz	½ cup
3 g	*Celery stalks, chopped*	3	½ cup
30 g	*Mushrooms, chopped*	1 oz	¼ cup
2	*Eggs, beaten*	2	2
30 g	*Ham, chopped*	1 oz	¼ cup
225 g	*Pork or fat*	8 oz	1 cup
225 g	*Puff pastry*	8 oz	8 oz
1	*Beaten egg to glaze*	1	1

1. Set the oven to 170°C, 325°F, Gas Mark 3.
2. Melt the butter in a pan and cook the carrots, onion and garlic until they are soft and the garlic begins to brown. Remove the garlic and discard.
3. Place the breadcrumbs in a basin and add the celery, mushrooms, eggs and ham. Season with salt and freshly ground black pepper and mix well.
4. Fill the lamb with the stuffing. Tie securely with string.
5. Spread the fat on top and bake for about 18 minutes per pound. When half baked, remove and allow to cool.
6. Roll out the pastry, remove the string and place the lamb in the centre. Cover with the pastry, brushing the edges with the egg to seal. Brush the top with the remaining egg.
7. Place on a greased baking tray and cook for up to an hour until the meat is tender and the pastry golden brown.

* *The shank bone may be left in, if preferred — Editor.*

LOIN OF PORK VICTORIA *Serves 2*

This pretty pork dish from the Hospitality Inn, Harrogate arrives at the table coated in a delicious creamy sauce and topped with fresh plums.

Metric		lb/oz	U.S.A.
	1½ kg (3 lb) Loin of pork, boned		
85 g	Flour	3 oz	⅔ cup
125 g	Butter	4 oz	½ cup
2	Small onions, chopped	2	1 cup
567 g	Plums, medium can of	1¼ lb	1¼ lb
600 ml	Double cream	1 pt	2 cups
75 ml	Demi-glace sauce (p. 75)*	⅛ pt	¼ cup
4 tsp	Redcurrant jelly	4 tsp	4 tsp
8	Fresh plums, stoned and quartered	8	8
2 tbsp	Chopped parsley	2 tbsp	2 tbsp

1. Slice the pork allowing two slices per person and flatten with a rolling pin. Season lightly and coat with the flour.
2. Melt the butter in a large pan and fry the pork on both sides for about 4 minutes. Remove and keep warm.
3. Add the onion to the pan and fry gently until transparent.
4. Drain the juice from the plums. Put them in the pan with 2 tbsp juice and the cream. Add the demi-glace and the redcurrant jelly. Bring to the boil then cook gently to reduce the liquid, stirring constantly.
5. Return the pork to the pan and simmer briefly. Remove to a warmed serving dish, and decorate with the fresh plums.
6. Season the sauce to taste and pour over the pork. Garnish with the parsley and serve immediately.

* *Gravy may be substituted — Editor.*

The Guilds

The medieval guilds were commercial brotherhoods established to protect the interests of their members. Each guild related to a specific profession or trade and offered its members, in exchange for a subscription, financial support during such times of misfortune as sickness or bereavement. Some guilds were also active in protecting their members from exploitation and injustice.

Many guilds in York were extremely prosperous and enjoyed considerable status in the city. Judging by the two surviving guild halls, which are impressive medieval buildings, a great deal of prestige was attached to these societies. Guilds also performed the ancient Mystery Plays, and would often enact a play connected with the profession of its members. The Mariners, for example, acted the story of Noah's Ark.

There are three guilds for local businessmen still in existence today — The Merchant Adventurers, The Merchant Taylors and The Butchers.

CARVED FACE IN YORK GUILDHALL: *This wonderfully grotesque face with its delightful, toothy grin is an original 15th century carving which survived the extensive damage to the Guildhall during the Second World War.*

THE YORK MYSTERY PLAYS

The famous dramatic cycle known as the York Mystery Plays was mainly derived from the 'Cursor Mundi' — an immensely long poem on religious history written in the reign of Edward II. The plays were originally performed annually on the festival of Corpus Christi, which was one of the great days in the medieval calendar.

The day's celebrations began at dawn when the actors assembled with their carts at Micklegate. Being a public holiday, the whole town would turn out to watch the performances. The performers would form themselves and their carts into a procession, and they would then follow a set route through the town.

Each trade guild was responsible for at least one play, which was performed twelve times — once at every stop. The plays were based on biblical stories and contained a strong moral message. With a total of fifty plays in the cycle, the performances often carried on until nightfall.

Revived in the early 1950's, the Mystery Plays are now performed every four years during York Festival in the grounds of St. Mary's Abbey.

THE GUILDHALL, YORK

York's Guildhall was the product of medieval civic co-operation, built as a joint venture between the Guild of St. Christopher and the Common Council. It survived, intact, into the twentieth century only to be severely damaged during the Second World War. However, careful attention to detail has resulted in a near perfect restoration.

Thankfully the Inner Chamber, which adjoins the Guildhall, escaped serious harm. Spot the secret doorways in the wooden panelling, and ponder on what shady dealings these were used for! This is the room in which £200,000 exchanged hands between the English Parliamentarians and the Scottish army in 1648 for the capture of King Charles I.

ESCALOPES DE VEAU SAVOYARDE
Serves 4

A brandy sauce and melted cheese topping make this contribution from Harrogate's Number 6 Restaurant quite irresistible.

Metric		lb/oz	U.S.A.
	4 Thin veal escalopes		
60 g	*Butter*	2 oz	¼ cup
1	*Onion, chopped*	1	½ cup
3 tbsp	*Flour*	3 tbsp	¼ cup
125 ml	*Brandy*	¼ pt	½ cup
300 ml	*Double cream*	½ pt	1 cup
125 g	*Gruyère cheese, grated*	4 oz	1 cup
4	*Parsley sprigs*	4	4

1. Melt half the butter in a pan and sauté the onion until transparent but not browned. Remove the onion with a draining spoon and purée in a liquidizer.
2. Season the escalopes with salt and pepper then coat with flour.
3. Add the remaining butter to the pan and sauté the escalopes for a few minutes on each side. Remove to a warm serving dish.
4. Remove any excess fat from the pan, pour in the brandy and boil until the liquid is reduced by half. Add the cream and cook gently until the sauce thickens.
5. Spread the onion purée on top of each escalope and sprinkle with cheese. Put under a hot grill for a few minutes to allow the cheese to melt.
6. To serve, pour the sauce over and decorate with parsley.

"I'll fill hup the chinks wi' cheese."

Handley Cross
R.S. SURTEES, 1803-1864

SALTIMBOCCA
Serves 6

This winning combination of sliced veal and ham cooked in a generous amount of Marsala wine comes from the Ristorante Bari.

Metric		lb/oz	U.S.A.
	12 Small veal escalopes		
	12 Small ham slices		
2 tbsp	*Lemon juice*	2 tbsp	2 tbsp
12	*Fresh sage leaves, (or 1 tsp dried sage)*	12	12
4 tbsp	*Butter*	4 tbsp	⅓ cup
125 ml	*Marsala*	4 fl oz	½ cup
	Fried bread croûtons to garnish		

1. Beat the escalopes with a rolling pin until very thin, then rub with lemon juice.
2. Lay a slice of ham and a leaf of sage on each slice of veal. Roll up and secure with a toothpick.
3. Melt the butter in a pan and add the escalopes. Season with salt and pepper then cook gently till brown all over.
4. Pour over the Marsala. Let it bubble for a minute then cover the pan and simmer until quite tender.
5. Remove the escalopes, taking out the toothpicks, and arrange on a warm serving dish. Pour over the sauce and serve with the croûtons.

The Coming of the Railway

York's huge railway station, built in 1877, is a fine and imposing building. Planners designed it in a great, sweeping curve to allow trains to arrive and depart with the greatest efficiency. It is a reminder of the important link between the railway and the City in the nineteenth century — a link which has not been broken; today the headquarters of British Rail's Eastern Region are in York.

Visitors who come to York by train — and particularly those who visit the famous **National Railway Museum** (which boasts two acres of locomotives dating from 1822 to 1902) — will be interested to learn how the railways came to York.

George Hudson, the Railway King

George Hudson was an enterprising draper's apprentice in York who did the traditional thing in marrying the boss's daughter and inheriting his fortune! He became a successful businessman and was attracted by the economic possibilities of the 'Railway Age'. He went to considerable personal trouble to encourage the railway companies to bring their lines to York, so boosting the town's economy by enormous trade. The whole project brought him such respect and esteem that he was nick-named 'The Railway King'. However, like many business magnates he came to a sorry end: he finally fled England to escape imprisonment for debts and died, still in exile, in 1871.

It cannot be doubted that Hudson did a great deal for York's prosperity by attracting the railways. His name, which had been given to 'Hudson Street' and then taken away as a result of the scandal, was later re-instated.

DOUBLE CRUST CHICKEN PIE   *Serves 4*

Which came first, the chicken or the egg? Take your pick
when you slice into this upper crust (!) version of an everyday
pie served by Chef Stuart Wynne at the Viking Hotel.

Metric		lb/oz	U.S.A.
	1 × 1.75 kg (3-4 lb) Chicken, cooked		
225 g	Streaky bacon	8 oz	8 oz
125 g	Button mushrooms, sliced	4 oz	1 cup
1	Bay leaf	1	1
1	Onion, chopped	1	½ cup
1	Chopped parsley, pinch of	1	1
1	Hard-boiled egg, chopped	1	1
300 ml	Chicken stock	½ pt	1 cup
225 g	Puff pastry	8 oz	8 oz
1	Egg, beaten	1	1

1. Remove the meat from the bones and cut into pieces about
   4 x 1 cm (1½ x ½"). Season with salt and pepper.
2. Wrap each piece of chicken in a thin strip of streaky bacon
   and place in a pie dish with the mushrooms, bay leaf,
   onion, parsley, egg and enough stock to barely cover the
   chicken.
3. Roll out the pastry, brush the edge of the pie dish with the
   beaten egg then cut strips of pastry to line the edge of the
   dish. Brush the pastry edge with egg.
4. Place the remaining pastry on top of the pie dish without
   stretching it, seal firmly then brush all over with the egg.
   Put in a cold place and leave to rest for about an hour. Set
   the oven to 200°C, 400°F, Gas Mark 6.
5. Bake on the centre shelf for ¾ hour until golden brown.

MICKLEGATE BAR, YORK

Micklegate Bar is one of the four gates of York commonly
called 'Bars'. They were originally strung with chains, and an
additional defence, or barbican, extended beyond. So there is
no alcoholic connotation! Walmgate Bar is the only one to
retain its barbican. The Bars' defensive role has disappeared
but they still dominate the major roads in and out of York.
It was at Micklegate that traitors' heads were displayed as a
gory warning. In 1460 the head of Richard of York was
exhibited, and after the Jacobite Rising of '45, the traitors'
heads were not removed for eight years!
In medieval times the Bars were guarded day and night, and
there was a drastic punishment for a guard found dozing three
times in succession: he would be placed in a basket with just a
knife and a small supply of bread and water, and suspended
over the moat into which the City's sewage and refuse were
drained. He could either starve or cut the rope, being banished
for a year and a day if he survived the murky waters!

CHICKEN CALYPSO *Serves 4*

... or chicken collapso depending on how much liqueur you add! The Viking Hotel recommend you stick to the amount they use and serve the chicken on a bed of rice.

Metric		lb/oz	U.S.A.
	1 x 2 kg (3-4 lb) Chicken		
60 g	Butter	2 oz	¼ cup
45 g	Flour	1½ oz	3 tbsp
600 ml	Chicken stock	1 pt	2½ cups
1 tbsp	Coffee essence	1 tbsp	1 tbsp
1–2 tbsp	Tia Maria, to taste	1–2 tbsp	1–2 tbsp
2	Egg yolks	2	2
4 tbsp	Double cream	4 tbsp	⅓ cup
2 tbsp	Parsley, chopped	2 tbsp	2 tbsp

1. Remove the meat from the bones of the chicken, cut into small pieces and season with salt and pepper.
2. Melt the butter in a pan over a gentle heat. Add the pieces of chicken and cover with a lid. Cook, turning once without browning the meat. Remove from the heat and stir in the flour.
3. Cook for a few minutes, then pour in the stock, stirring constantly; bring to the boil and skim off any fat. Reduce the heat.
4. Add the essence and Tia Maria. Simmer gently until the chicken is tender.
5. Put the yolks in a basin and stir in the cream. Mix well.
6. Remove the chicken from the stock, place on a serving dish and keep warm. Pour a little of the stock on to the egg yolks and return them to the pan. Heat through, stirring all the time, but do not boil. Check the seasoning.
7. Pour the sauce over the chicken, sprinkle with the parsley and serve immediately.

STONEGATE AND THE MANSION HOUSE, YORK *(overleaf)*
A highway rather than a gateway, Stonegate probably derives its name from 'gate', the Old Norse word for street and from the fact that in Roman times it was the via praetoria (main street) which was paved with stone. Stonegate's links with the past are many — this route is known to have been a highway for almost nineteen hundred years and contains architecture from just about every age from Norman to Victorian, including a house in which Guy Fawkes' parents lived.
At the end of Stonegate looms the stately Georgian elegance of the Mansion House. Built in 1725, it is still the Lord Mayor's residence during his term of office. Another Mansion House tradition that has not changed is the serving of dinner by candlelight, in keeping with eighteenth century custom.

POUSSIN ROTI AU CHAMPAGNE   *Serves 4*

For those with something to celebrate, a cream and champagne chicken extravaganza from the Number 6 Restaurant, Harrogate.

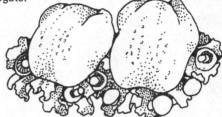

Metric		lb/oz	U.S.A.
	4 x 350-400 g (12-14 oz) Baby chickens		
125 g	*Button mushrooms, sliced*	4 oz	1 cup
375 ml	*Champagne or sparkling white wine*	12 fl. oz	1¼ cups
300 ml	*Double cream*	½ pt	1 cup
4 tbsp	*Chopped parsley*	4 tbsp	⅓ cup

1. Set the oven to 200°C, 400°F, Gas Mark 6.
2. Season the chickens, and place in a roasting tin for up to 25 minutes until tender.
3. Remove the chickens, place on a serving dish and keep warm. Drain off any excess liquid.
4. Sauté the mushrooms in the roasting tin. Drain off any excess fat, add the champagne and bring to the boil. Boil to reduce the liquid until just a few spoonfuls remain.
5. Stir in the cream and heat gently until the mixture starts to thicken. Pour over the chickens and sprinkle with parsley.

TOO MUCH CHAMPAGNE *might cause you to see pink elephants, but sometimes strange things can be seen without the assistance of alcohol! York has its share of fantastic ghost stories, but one about the Roman Legion is particularly striking. A local plumber working in the cellars of the Treasurer's House behind York Minster was enjoying his lunch break, when his seclusion was interrupted by a troop of Roman foot soldiers! As the plumber watched, amazed, they marched in through one wall and out by another! The factor which particularly seizes the imagination is that while he was able to give a detailed description of the men, he claimed not to have been able to see below their knees since these were obscured by the cellar floor. Later excavations revealed the remains of a Roman road approximately 18" below the present foundations!*

STONEGATE AND THE MANSION HOUSE, YORK
(see previous page)

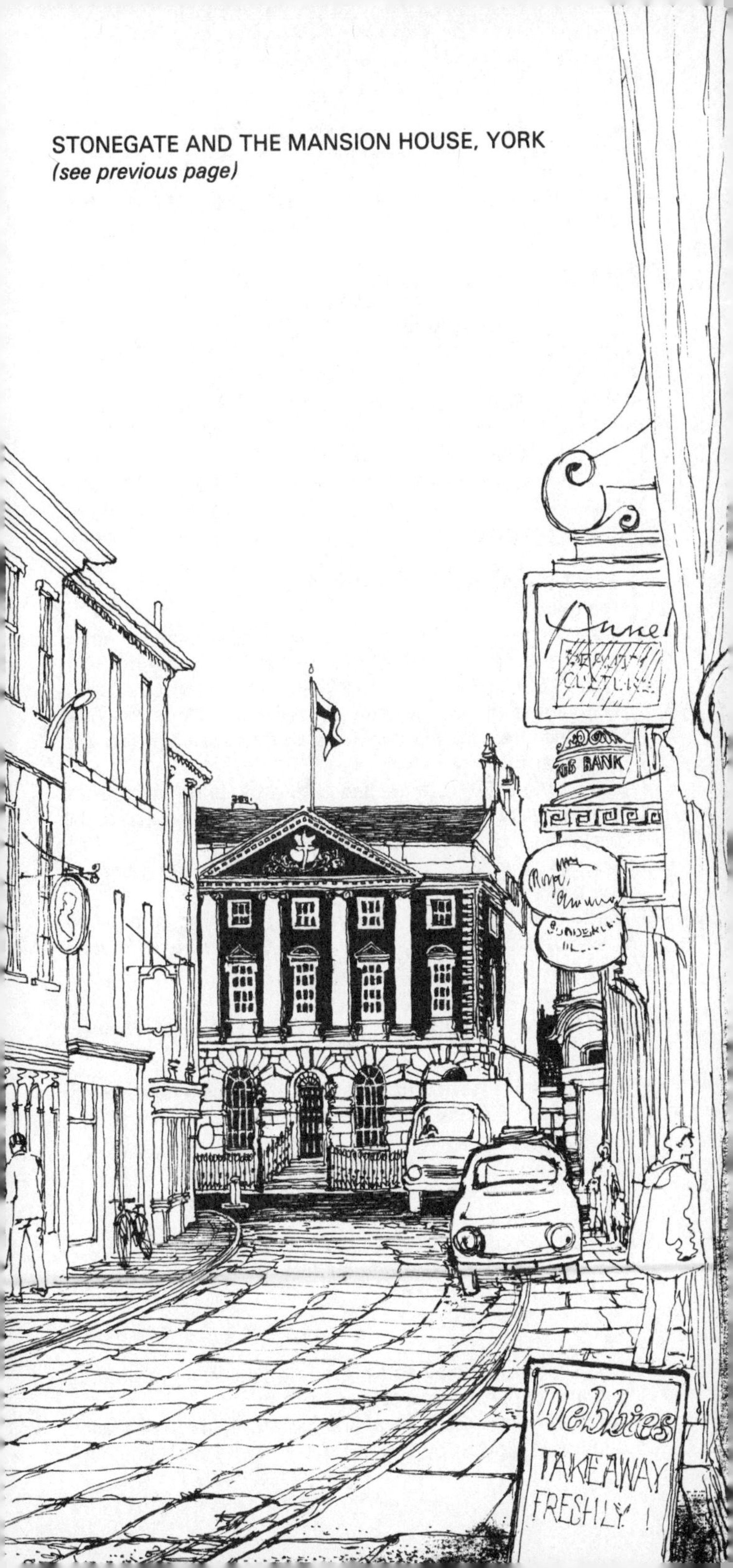

TIPSY DUCK WITH VEAL STUFFING   *Serves 2*

A wickedly delicious poultry treat from the Hotel Majestic, Harrogate.

Metric		lb/oz	U.S.A.
	1 × 1 kg (2 lb) Duck		
175 g	Rice, cooked	6 oz	¾ cup
175 g	Veal, minced	6 oz	¾ cup
30 g	Green pepper, diced	1 oz	¼ cup
60 g	Butter, softened	2 oz	¼ cup
75 ml	Double cream	⅛ pt	¼ cup
1	Onion, chopped	1	½ cup
150 ml	White wine	¼ pt	½ cup
1 tbsp	Beef stock	1 tbsp	1 tbsp
150 ml	Brandy	¼ pt	½ cup

1. Set the oven to 200°C, 400°F, Gas Mark 6. Wash and dry the duck.
2. To make the stuffing, place the rice, veal and green pepper in a bowl and stir well. Bind with a little of the butter and cream. Season with salt and freshly ground black pepper.
3. Stuff the duck and place in a roasting tin. Cook for 45-50 minutes. Transfer the duck to a warmed serving dish and keep warm.
4. Skim off any fat from the pan juices, and bring them to the boil, reducing by half. Add 1 tsp butter and the onion to the pan. Replace in the oven to finish cooking.
5. Pour in the wine, 2 tsp cream and the stock. Bring back to the boil and cook gently until further reduced by half.
6. Season to taste, add the brandy, remaining butter and cream and heat through. Pour over the duck and serve.

MOUSSELINE OF TURKEY   *Serves 4*

From Hodgson's Restaurant, Harrogate, a recipe for turkey in a sauce which sounds as though it should set you singing!

Metric		lb/oz	U.S.A.
	4 × 125 g (4 oz) Turkey breasts		
2	Eggs, separated	2	2
85 ml	Double cream	3 fl. oz	⅓ cup
	For the poaching liquid:		
300 ml	Milk	½ pt	1 cup
2	Bay leaves	2	2

1. Chop the raw turkey and place in a liquidizer with a little salt and pepper. Blend to a smooth purée.
2. Add one egg white at a time, blending between each addition, followed by the two yolks. Blend well together.

3. Pour the mixture into a bowl and chill this and the cream thoroughly (refrigerate for 2 hours or deep freeze for 20 minutes).
4. When completely cold remove from the refrigerator and beat the cream into the turkey and egg mixture by hand. Season to taste. Return to the refrigerator and chill for two hours.
5. Put the milk, with two cups of water and the bay leaves in a large pan with a pinch of salt. Bring to the boil then turn the heat down until the liquid is just simmering.
6. When the turkey mixture has set, remove from the refrigerator and, using a large warm spoon, scoop out the mousseline to form egg shapes. Place each one in the simmering liquid to poach.
7. Allow 2 per person and cook for 4 minutes on each side. Do not allow the liquid to boil. Remove with a straining spoon allowing each one to drain well.
8. Place on a serving dish and cover with the sauce.

'Song Thrush' sauce

½ tsp	Black peppercorns, crushed	½ tsp	½ tsp
2 tbsp	White wine vinegar	2 tbsp	2 tbsp
2	Shallots, chopped	2	2
150 g	Butter	5½ oz	⅔ cup
3	Egg yolks	3	3
60 g	White button mushrooms, chopped	2 oz	½ cup
2 tbsp	Port	2 tbsp	2 tbsp
2 tbsp	Double cream	2 tbsp	2 tbsp
2 tsp	Tarragon, chopped	2 tsp	2 tsp
1	Nutmeg, pinch of	1	1

1. Put the peppercorns, wine vinegar and half of the shallots into a pan and bring to the boil. Cook until the liquid has reduced by three-quarters.
2. Clarify all but 2 tsp of the butter, (see p.76).
3. Place the egg yolks in a bowl with 1 tsp water and a pinch of salt and beat well. Strain into the vinegar and shallots.
4. Beat the mixture with a small whisk over a pan of boiling water until the yolks have made 'ribbons' in the mixture. Carefully whisk in the butter a little at a time.
5. Melt the remaining butter in a small pan and cook the remaining shallots until transparent.
6. Add the mushrooms and cook for 2-3 minutes. Add the port and bring to the boil until the liquid is reduced by half.
7. Remove from the heat, add 1 tbsp cream and the tarragon. Season with salt and black pepper and stir in the nutmeg.
8. Blend the vinegar and mushroom mixtures together until you have a smooth, shiny sauce. Check the seasoning and beat in the remaining cream.

PAELLA DE MARISCOS

Add a carafe of Sangria and some melancholy guitar players to the setting when serving this delightful dish, and you could be in Spain instead of Harrogate! A contribution from Emilio's Restaurant.

Metric		lb/oz	U.S.A.
	1 Small chicken cut into 8 pieces		
125 ml	Dry white wine	4 fl. oz	½ cup
24	Mussels, cleaned and bearded	24	24
150 ml	Olive oil	¼ pt	½ cup
2-3	Garlic cloves, chopped	2-3	2-3
1	Large onion, chopped	1	1 cup
1	Red pepper, de-seeded and cut into strips	1	1
1 tsp	Paprika	1 tsp	1 tsp
250 g	Fish*	8 oz	1½ cups
4	Tomatoes, peeled and chopped	4	2 cups
225 g	Long grain rice	8 oz	1 cup
½ tsp	Saffron	½ tsp	½ tsp
600 ml	Chicken stock	1 pt	2½ cups
125 g	Peas	4 oz	½ cup
175 g	Shelled prawns	6 oz	1 cup
175 g	Unshelled prawns	6 oz	1 cup
125 g	Olives	4 oz	½ cup
8	Lemon wedges	8	8

* Use monk fish or scampi or any hard white fish cut into pieces.

SPAIN *may have been famous for its explorers, but so is York.* **Captain Cook** *started his professional career at the age of 12 apprenticed to a haberdashery business in Great Auton, Yorkshire where he was schooled and grew up. His imagination was fired by hearing of* **Wolfe's** *capture of Quebec, and he ran away to sea to embark on some adventures of his own. His plucky sense of adventure took him around the world and he went on to navigate the Great Barrier Reef and to discover New Zealand.*

Captain Cook *was not only a great explorer, but was also something of an early dietician. It is believed that none of his crew suffered from scurvy because be became aware of the need for vitamin C and saw to it that fresh fruit and vegetables were taken on board.*

The Black Swan *was originally a private house. In the seventeenth century it was the childhood home of Henrietta Thompson, who was later to become the mother of* **General James Wolfe,** *hero of Quebec.*

1. Place the wine and mussels (only use those that are tightly closed) in a shallow pan. Boil gently until the mussels open, discard any that do not open. Remove the mussels and keep warm. Drain the juice into a separate bowl.
2. Heat the oil and garlic in the pan and cook gently until golden in colour. Remove the garlic and discard. Add the onion and peppers and chicken pieces. Sprinkle the chicken with the paprika. Cook gently, stirring constantly for 10 minutes.
3. Add the fish pieces and the tomatoes. Stir well. Heat through.
4. Stir in the rice and cook for 2 minutes. Add the saffron, stock, peas and juice set aside from the wine and mussels. Bring to the boil and season with salt and pepper.
5. Set the oven to 150°C, 300°F Gas Mark 2.
6. Stir the shelled prawns into the mixture and cook gently for 15 minutes or until all the liquid has been absorbed.
7. Place in an ovenproof dish, and decorate the paella with mussels, unshelled prawns and olives. Place in the oven for 10 minutes.
8. Serve in the same dish garnished with lemon wedges.

Highwaymen & Hangings

Dick Turpin, surely the most famous and romanticised highwayman of all time, was convicted in York as a highwayman in 1739.

In 1676, another highwayman called **William Nerison** robbed a man at Gad's Hill near Chatham. He then rode furiously all the way to York, arriving in the late afternoon. He went straight to the bowling green on the Knavesmire, and took great care to make a lasting impression on the Lord Mayor by speaking outrageously. When brought to court, he was acquitted on the Lord Mayor's identification — the court deciding it was impossible for him to have been in two places at once!

York gallows were originally situated on open ground outside the City, but the crowds so seriously hindered trade and transport that the gallows were moved to a new site behind the Castle. It was hoped that the restricted views would discourage people from coming, but as late as 1862 special excursion trains were bringing sightseers from rural districts to York for the hangings! Given a good programme, the crowd would sometimes number ten thousand — with street sellers and strolling players helping to create a holiday atmosphere!

York Minster

From all around York the Gothic towers of the Minster are the focal point of the City, rising high above the picturesque shops and houses. It is hardly surprising that the towers are so imposing since the pair which greet the visitor who approaches the west doors are 196 feet high, only two feet lower than the massive Central Tower with its 275 steps.

Simple beginnings

The first church to be built on the site was a simple wooden structure erected in A.D. 627 for the baptism of King Edwin of Northumbria, when he became a convert to Christianity. The present Minster is the fifth church to stand on the site, taking 250 years to build, and giving employment to the area's leading craftsmen all that time. It was finally consecrated in 1472.

Medieval treasures

York Minster is not only the largest medieval Gothic cathedral in Europe, but also contains the greatest concentration of medieval stained glass. The two most famous windows are the 'Five Sisters' and the Great East Window.

The Great East Window covers two thousand square feet and is thought to be the largest area of medieval stained glass in the world. It was St. Wilfred (634-709) who, as Bishop of Northumbria, was originally responsible for glazing the Minster. He would no doubt have approved of the conservationists who spent twenty years piecing together all the glass removed for safety in 1939.

The 'Five Sisters' probably takes its name from the five graceful arches. There are, however, a number of more romantic interpretations including one from Charles Dickens in 'Nicholas Nickleby'. He tells of five sisters who lived in York and worked tapestries of rare and delicate beauty. When Alice, the youngest sister, died, the others had the tapestries transformed into stained glass as a mark of their sorrow.

Continued overleaf

YORK MINSTER

Seen from this angle, the Minster presents a lovely confusion of intricate stonework and delicate engraving. It is a vast building — the largest Gothic church in England. Its lofty heights command a view of the town from a site which has always been one of the most important in York. Originally, the Roman Principia or military headquarters were situated here. Later in 627 A.D. the first church was built entirely of wood. Today the familiar stone towers can be seen dominating the skyline from points all around the city.

The Rose window, high above the doorway, is mainly sixteenth century glass. Its red and white roses (red for Lancaster, white for York) commemorate the peaceful ending of the War of the Roses when Henry (VII) of Lancaster married Elizabeth of York in 1486.

Turbulent times

Richard Scrope (1350-1405) was one of the most famous Archbishops of York. His family were amongst the Minster's chief benefactors, and their Coat of Arms, a blue shield with a gold 'bend' crossing it diagonally, is to be seen in the Cathedral. Nonetheless, on the Feast of St. William of York, he was executed for taking part in an uprising against Henry IV. In 1829 his tomb was opened, revealing his head placed neatly under his arm!

Big Peter

If you are anywhere near the Minster at noon, you will hear the sound of Big Peter, the Minster's largest bell. Weighing eleven tons, the bell was brought to York in 1845 by train. After it had been hung, it was discovered that thirty men would be needed to set it swinging, so a hammer was installed. Then it was found to be out of tune with the rest of the peal! The inspired solution was that it should be limited to a solo performance at noon daily.

Preserved for posterity

The Minster has survived two serious fires. The choirstalls were set on fire in 1829, and in 1840 the south west tower was destroyed, causing the bells to crash to the ground. But in spite of accidents, religious upheavals, riots and wars, the Minster has survived. It is the only cathedral outside the Vatican in Rome to boast an ecclesiastical police force, whose uniforms display the Crossed Keys of St. Peter. There is, however, some doubt as to the force's ability to defend the cathedral effectively in a crisis, as it consists of only four officers!

THE CHANCEL, YORK MINSTER

On either side of the High Altar, at the ends of the choir screens are two statues. One is the eleventh century King Edwin who built the very first church on this site and the other is Edward VII depicted in his coronation robes.
King Edwin was converted to Christianity and in A.D. 627 was baptised in a tiny church built especially for the occasion. He can fairly be accredited with the first and perhaps most important step in York's long ecclesiastical history.
The lovely stained glass of the Great East Window is as beautiful today as when it was completed in 1408. It took a Coventry man, John Thornton, three years to design and make the panels and for his work he was paid the (then) princely sum of £56!

CANESTRELLA ALLA CREMA

Serves 6

The Ristorante Bari has created this rice dish especially for shellfish and white wine aficionados.

Metric		lb/oz	U.S.A.
	1 kg (2 lb) Queen (small) scallops		
225 g	*Rice, long grain*	8 oz	1 cup
3 tbsp	*Oil*	3 tbsp	¼ cup
125 ml	*White wine*	4 fl. oz	½ cup
1	*Parsley sprig, chopped*	1	1
150 ml	*Whipping cream*	¼ pt	½ cup

1. Cook the rice in boiling salted water until tender.
2. Heat the oil in a large pan and gently fry the scallops. Pour away the surplus oil and add the wine. Season with a pinch of salt and some freshly ground black pepper. Sprinkle with a pinch of parsley. Add the cream and stir-fry gently.
3. Strain the rice in a colander and pour boiling water over to separate the grains. Shake to drain, then transfer to a warm serving dish, making a well in the centre. Spoon in the scallops and garnish with the remaining parsley.

THE CHAPTER HOUSE, YORK MINSTER *(see also p.5)*

Looking up at this beautiful vaulted wooden ceiling with its golden stars on a blue background, architecture buffs will see that it seems to defy all structural principles — it is an octagonal building with no central pillar. In these days of re-inforced concrete this may not seem surprising but, built in the 13th century it really is a considerable architectural feat!

Nowadays the Chapter House displays some of the Minster's treasures, but originally it was built as a Council Chamber or meeting place for the Dean and Chapter, the governing body of the Minster. Perhaps the carving by the doorway, of the Virgin Mary treading on a dragon, hints at the tone of these policy making meetings!

Inside, the beauty of this unusual octagonal room is summed up by an inscription on the wall: *"As the rose is the flower of flowers so this is the house of houses."*

ARCHBISHOP ROGER'S CRYPT

The Minster's crypt is named after Roger of Pont l'Evêque, who was Archbishop of York between 1154 and 1181.

THE UNDERCROFT *is a miracle of modern engineering, constructed of concrete rafts and stainless steel rods erected underneath the Minster in the early 1970's to save the building from collapse.*

SMOKED HADDOCK MOUSSE

*Serves 2 as a main dish
or 4–6 as a starter*

St. William's Restaurant in York have contributed this creamy fish mousse which is both inexpensive and easy to create.

Metric		lb/oz	U.S.A.
225 g	Smoked haddock, cooked and flaked	8 oz	1½ cups
300 ml	Béchamel sauce (see p. 76)	½ pt	1 cup
150 ml	Mayonnaise	¼ pt	½ cup
15 g	Gelatine	½ oz	1½ leaves
85 ml	Stock or water	⅛ pt	¼ cup
85 ml	Double cream	⅛ pt	¼ cup
2	Eggs, hard-boiled and chopped	2	2
	Cucumber slices to garnish		

1. Cool the béchamel sauce and mix with the mayonnaise.
2. Soak the gelatine in the stock or water and dissolve over a gentle heat. Add to the sauce mixture. Whip cream lightly.
3. Stir in the haddock and eggs and as the mixture begins to thicken fold in the cream.
4. Turn into a serving dish and chill until set.
5. Garnish with cucumber slices.

SALMON WITH CHAMPAGNE SAUCE

Serves 4

Salmon and asparagus are two of the best matched foods. Coated in champagne sauce, a mouthwatering creation is guaranteed. This dish is served to diners by Richard Hodgson of Hodgson's Restaurant.

Metric		lb/oz	U.S.A.
	4 x 125 g (4 oz) Salmon fillets, skinned and boned		
8	Fresh, large-tipped asparagus spears	8	8
60 g	Butter	2 oz	¼ cup
60 g	Shallots, chopped	2 oz	½ cup
300 ml	Sparkling wine	½ pt	1 cup
225 ml	Double cream	⅓ pt	¾ cup

"Champagne certainly gives one werry gentlemanly ideas, but for a continuance, I don't know but I should prefer mild hale."

Jorrock's Jaunts and Jollities
R.S. SURTEES, 1803-1864

1. Place the fillets between two pieces of foil and flatten with a meat hammer or rolling pin until about 1 cm (½") thick. Season with salt and pepper.
2. Cook the asparagus standing in salted, boiling water until tender and keep warm.
3. Using a non-stick frying pan quickly cook each salmon escalope in turn, one minute each side*. Place on a warm serving dish.
4. Using the same pan, melt half the butter and cook the shallots until they are tender but not browned.
5. Pour over the wine, bring to the boil and boil until the liquid is reduced to a quarter.
6. Add the cream and boil gently, stirring the remaining butter in until a coating consistency is reached. Season to taste and keep warm.
7. Split the asparagus heads lengthwise, arrange neatly on top of the escalopes. Pour the champagne sauce over and serve.

* Use minimum fat if a non-stick pan is not available — Editor.

SPAGHETTI ALLA VONGOLE　　　　　　　　　　*Serves 6*

Fancy a change from spaghetti bolognaise? If you like seafood, you will love this recipe from the chefs of the Ristorante Bari who tells us it is a favourite with their customers.

Metric		lb/oz	U.S.A.
450 g	Spaghetti	1 lb	1 lb
2 tbsp	Olive oil	2 tbsp	2 tbsp
2	Onions, finely chopped	2	1 cup
2	Garlic cloves, crushed	2	2
450 g	Tomatoes*, chopped	1 lb	2 cups
200 g	Clams or cockles, tinned or fresh	7 oz	7 oz
2 tsp	Sugar	2 tsp	2 tsp
1 tsp	Basil or parsley, chopped	1 tsp	1 tsp

1. Ease the spaghetti into a pan of boiling, salted water and cook for about 10—12 minutes or until 'al dente', which means cooked but not too soft.
2. While the spaghetti is cooking, heat the oil in a large pan and sauté the onion and garlic. Add the tomatoes, season with salt and freshly ground black pepper and simmer.
3. Add the clams or cockles (chopped if preferred), sugar and basil and stir well over a gentle heat.
4. Drain the spaghetti and divide between individual bowls. Coat with clam sauce and serve immediately.

* Tinned, skinned and chopped if fresh.

> "And when they were up they were up,
> And when they were down they were down,
> And when they were only half way up,
> They were neither up nor down."

A description of soufflés? No! It's the second verse of that well known 18th century nursery rhyme which begins . . .

> **"The grand old Duke of York,**
> He had ten thousand men,
> He marched them up to the top of the hill,
> And he marched them down again."

If he were around today, the Grand Old Duke would think it well worth climbing the hill to Harrogate's Majestic Hotel to enjoy their shellfish soufflé. It's quite a challenge for any cook to serve this mouthwatering treat while it's still puffed up! So make sure your guests are ready and waiting.

Metric		lb/oz	U.S.A.
225 ml	*Double cream*	⅓ pt	¾ cup
2	*Eggs, separated*	2	2
125 g	*Parmesan cheese, grated*	4 oz	1 cup
3 tbsp	*Swiss cheese, grated*	3 tbsp	¼ cup
125 g	*Cooked crab or lobster meat*	4 oz	⅔ cup
2 tbsp	*Brandy*	2 tbsp	2 tbsp
1	*Cayenne pepper, pinch of*	1	1
30 g	*Butter*	1 oz	2 tbsp

1. Set the oven to 190°C, 375°F, Gas Mark 5.
2. Pour the cream into a bowl and whip until firm but not too stiff. Mix in the egg yolks, half the Parmesan cheese, the Swiss cheese, shellfish, brandy, a pinch of salt and the cayenne pepper.
3. Place the egg whites in a clean, dry bowl and whisk until firm and stiff. Fold gently into the egg yolk mixture.
4. Butter four individual soufflé dishes and sprinkle with half the remaining Parmesan cheese. Fill each dish almost to the brim with the egg and cheese mixture, sprinkle the remaining Parmesan cheese on the top of each one.
5. Bake in the oven for 8–10 minutes. When golden brown serve immediately; as there is no flour in the mixture the soufflé will not stay puffed for many minutes after it has left the oven.

NEW YORK, NEW YORK *American visitors would be quite right to imagine that their famous city derives its name from a York connection. In 1644 the British captured it from the Dutch and renamed it in honour of James Stuart, Duke of York and Albany who became James II.*

Royal York

Because of its strategic position, control of York has been vital to rulers of Britain throughout the ages. As far back as 306 A.D., **Constantine the Great** was declared Emperor by his troops in Eboracum (the Roman name for York), and the head of his statue may be seen in the Yorkshire Museum.

Harold Godwinson — the King Harold of '1066' fame — was in York celebrating the defeat of Scandinavian invaders when he heard that a certain Duke William of Normandy had invaded in the south. Harold and his followers marched south, arriving in a state of exhaustion, and were defeated at the Battle of Hastings. William the Conqueror subsequently took his revenge on the unfortunate citizens of York for their support of Harold.

Edward III brought his government to York in 1332 and it became the seat of government for the next five years. Visitors to the Minster's Lady Chapel will see Edward featured in its stained glass windows.

> THE TUDOR ROSE *symbolizes the union of the two English factions which fought so bitterly against each other during the Wars of the Roses. When Henry Tudor (representing the Lancastrians) came to the throne becoming Henry VII he married Elizabeth of York thus uniting the two noble families and their emblems, the red rose of Lancaster and the white rose of York. On the birth of their first son, Prince Arthur, they were merged to form the striped Tudor Rose.*

The Royal House of York

Our present Royal family have strong connections with York. Before the abdication of his brother, Edward VIII, **George VI** was Duke of York, and his wife (now **The Queen Mother**) was Duchess of York. This followed the tradition that the monarch's second son be given this title.

Continued on page 58 . . .

THE HERBERTS OF YORK *were a well known local family and staunch Monarchists. Sir Thomas Herbert, whose house can still be seen in The Pavement, became a great friend of Charles I and demonstrated his loyalty by actually staying with him the night before his execution, accompanying him on to the scaffold the following morning.*

THE KING'S MANOR, YORK

The peaceful medieval aspect of the King's Manor belies its former importance as the hot seat of political power in the North. During the fifteenth and sixteenth centuries the King's Manor housed the Council of the North — legal and administrative intermediary between London and the Northern Counties. The Coat of Arms on the front dates from the time when the President of the Council was the Earl of Strafford, nicknamed Black Tom Tyrant. However, in 1641, Black Tom was executed for his tyranny and the southern Parliament effectively curbed York's political independence.

58

Continued from page 55 . . .

The first Duke

The fourth son of Edward III, **Edmund Langley**, was the first Duke of York, and his brother John of Gaunt was Duke of Lancaster. From the death of Richard II until their union in 1468, the Royal Houses of York and Lancaster were pitched against each other in a series of power struggles. It was a bloody time in English history but because the combatants' emblems were the white rose of York and the red rose of Lancaster, this unhappy time has become known by the unlikely title of the Wars of the Roses.

The Wars of the Roses

In 1460 the Lancastrian King **Henry VI** defeated Richard Duke of York at Wakefield, and displayed his severed head on Micklegate Bar. Within a year, however, Richard's son toppled Henry and was crowned **Edward IV** in the Minster. The struggle did not end there. Warwick the Kingmaker, who had been Edward's powerful ally, defected to the Lancastrians in 1470, leading a coup against Edward and restoring Henry! But York's fortunes rose again. Edward was returned to power and after his death his brother the Duke of York became **Richard III**. He is said to have been popular with the people of York, and local people still tend to disbelieve that he was the heinous murderer of his two nephews, the little princes in the tower, as Shakespeare would have us believe.

Henry Tudor, though not a direct Lancastrian descendant, led their challenge at the Battle of Bosworth. Having defeated Richard, he ended the Wars of the Roses by marrying the Yorkists' remaining claimant. The white rose of York and the red rose of Lancaster were thus united in the Tudor rose of **Henry VII** and **Elizabeth of York.**

The Grand Old Duke of York

No summary of Royal York would be complete without a reference to this famous nursery rhyme character (see page 54). Frederick, George III's second son, was commander of the English army in Flanders and the rhyme derides his abortive operations against the French. Apart from the fact that the Duke was only 31, led 30,000 men and there was (so far as we can establish) no hill, the rhyme is fair comment! The unfortunate Frederick was also referred to by children in the eighteenth century when they called 'Duke or Darling' instead of 'heads or tails'. It came about because of his scandalous affair with Mrs. Mary Anne Clarke!

A Royal Wedding in York Minster

In a break from the tradition whereby Royal Weddings take place in Westminster Abbey, the present Duke and Duchess of Kent were married in York Minster in 1961.

WHOLE LEMON SOLE STUFFED
WITH CRABMEAT

Serves 8

A lovely light dinner dish from the Hospitality Inn, Harrogate. It is served in the Oliver Twist Refectory. (Yes, we're sure that he would have asked for more!).

Metric		lb/oz	U.S.A.
	8 Lemon sole		
150 g	Butter	5 oz	⅔ cup
2	Onions, chopped	2	1 cup
3 tbsp	Brandy	3 tbsp	¼ cup
300 ml	White wine	½ pt	1 cup
600 ml	Double cream	1 pt	2 cups
400 g	Lobster bisque, can	14 oz	14 oz
1 tsp	Chopped parsley	1 tsp	1 tsp
200 g	Crabmeat, dark	6 oz	1 cup
3 tbsp	Béchamel sauce (see p. 76)	3 tbsp	¼ cup
2 tsp	Paprika	2 tsp	2 tsp
4 tbsp	Flour	4 tbsp	⅓ cup
	Lemon wedges and		
	chopped cucumber to garnish		

"I sometimes dig for buttered rolls,
Or set limed twigs for crabs ... "

The Walrus and the Carpenter
Through the Looking-Glass
LEWIS CARROLL, 1832-1898

1. To make the sauce, melt a knob of butter in a pan and fry the onions lightly. Add the brandy and flambé.
2. Pour on the wine, cream and lobster bisque, and sprinkle with parsley.
3. Bring to the boil and cook gently (so that the sauce does not separate) until the liquid is reduced and the sauce thickens. Season with salt and pepper and keep warm.
4. Set the oven to 230°C, 450°F, Gas Mark 8.
5. Mix the crabmeat, béchamel and paprika together and season well.
6. Trim and remove the dark skin and head from the sole (your fishmonger will do this for you if you ask him). Make an incision about 8 cm (3") long down the back of each fish and take the flesh away from the bone for about 1 cm (½") on each side. Stuff the cavity with the crabmeat mixture.
7. Flour and season the sole on both sides and place in a buttered, ovenproof dish with the stuffed side on top.
8. Brush the sole with a little sauce and dot with the remaining butter. Cover with foil. Bake for 15—20 minutes or until tender, removing the foil after about 10 minutes to brown the fish.
9. Coat with sauce and garnish with lemon wedges at each end and cucumber sprinkled down the middle.

LOBSTER PRINCESS

Serves 4

For princes, too, an aromatic combination of lobster, spinach, brandy and port from Hodgson's Restaurant.

Metric		lb/oz	U.S.A.
	1 Lobster, freshly cooked (live weight 1 kg, 2 lb)		
12	Spinach leaves	12	12
85 g	Butter	3 oz	⅓ cup
2	Shallots, chopped	2 oz	½ cup
1	Leek, cut into small strips	1	1
1	Carrot, cut into small strips	1	1
3 tbsp	Brandy	3 tbsp	¼ cup
3 tbsp	Port	3 tbsp	¼ cup
125 g	Concentrated lobster soup*	4 fl oz	½ cup
100 ml	Double cream	3 fl oz	⅓ cup

1. Remove the meat and cut into 2 cm (1") pieces.
2. Bring a little water to the boil and blanch the spinach leaves for 2 minutes. Transfer to warmed soup dishes.
3. Heat the butter in a pan and cook the shallots until tender but not coloured. Add the leeks and carrots and cook for another 2 minutes. Add the lobster meat and cook gently for a further 2 minutes.
4. Pour over the brandy and port and flambe. Add the sauce.
5. Bring the liquid to the boil and cook gently to reduce. Stir in the cream, continue to cook gently to a coating consistency and season to taste.
6. Spoon the lobster and vegetables over the spinach, and pour over the sauce.

* The chef makes his own sauce.

THE MERCHANT ADVENTURERS' GATEWAY, YORK

This Fossgate entrance, dating from the seventeenth century, is younger than the rest of the Hall, but the motto above the doorway is appropriate to the whole of the guild's history: God give us good luck!

THE MIDDLE AGES was a time of great prosperity for merchants, as the number of fine, surviving medieval buildings in York goes to prove. The Merchant Adventurers' Hall (see also page 64) was built in 1361 when York was an important wool exporting town. Samples were weighed here before being shipped to Europe. The impressive building and guild name conjure up images of scheming merchants in fur-lined robes speculating on the price of wool! In reality, it seems they were excellent judges of their trade because the Guild was the undisputed ruler of the City in the fifteenth and sixteenth centuries.

Desserts and teatime treats

"Stolen sweets are best!"

The Rival Fools, Act 1
COLLEY CIBBER, 1671-1757

CHOCOLATE CHEESE DREAM   *Serves 4*

Did Mr Rowntree or Mr Terry ever eat a dessert as luscious? Joseph would certainly not have approved of adding orange liqueur! But we think it's definitely the stuff that dreams are made of.

Metric		lb/oz	U.S.A.
250 g	Cream cheese	8 oz	1 cup
50 g	Caster sugar	2 oz	4 tbsp
3	Eggs, separated	3	3
450 ml	Double cream	¾ pt	1 ½ cups
50 g	Mixed nuts, finely chopped	2 oz	½ cup
2 tbsp	Grand Marnier	2 tbsp	3 tbsp
125 g	Dark chocolate	4 oz	4 oz
	Sponge fingers to serve		

1. Place the cream cheese in a basin with the sugar and beat until the mixture is light and creamy.
2. Continue beating and slowly add the egg yolks to the mixture. Whip the cream and fold in with the nuts and Grand Marnier.
3. Reserve two squares of chocolate for decoration and place the remainder in a bowl. Melt over a pan of hot water. Stir gently until the chocolate has melted. Allow to cool then stir into the cheese mixture.
4. Whip the egg whites until they are stiff and stand in peaks then fold into the chocolate mixture. Pour into a large serving dish and chill in the refrigerator overnight.
5. Before serving, flake the remainder of the chocolate, using a potato peeler, over the centre of the dish. Serve with sponge fingers.

CHOCOLATE REFRIGERATOR GATEAU — *Serves 8*

Wicked, rich and wonderful — who could ask for more?

Metric		lb/oz	U.S.A.
250 g	*Dark chocolate*	8 oz	8 oz
3 tbsp	*Golden syrup*	3 tbsp	4 tbsp
150 g	*Butter*	6 oz	1 cup
300 g	*Digestive biscuits*	12 oz	12 oz
2 tsp	*Cinnamon*	2 tsp	2 tsp
50 g	*Sultanas*	2 oz	¼ cup
50 g	*Raisins*	2 oz	¼ cup
50 g	*Glacé cherries*	2 oz	¼ cup
2 tbsp	*Brandy*	2 tbsp	3 tbsp
300 ml	*Cream*	½ pt	1 cup

1. Place the chocolate, golden syrup and butter in a saucepan and melt over a low heat, stirring all the time.
2. Put the biscuits into a polythene bag, tie the end and crush with a rolling pin. Add the crushed biscuits and the cinnamon to the melted butter and mix well.
3. Add the sultanas, raisins, glacé cherries and brandy. Stir well.
4. Spoon into a large greased pudding basin, smooth the top and refrigerate.
5. When set, stand briefly in hot water to unmould then turn out on to a serving plate. Serve with cream.

CHOCOLATE LOVERS UNITE! *But not in York!! The famous firms of* **Terry's** *and* **Rowntree's** *still retain their own identities. Terry's shop has been reconstructed — complete with smells — in the Castle Museum. The Rowntree business was originally begun by the Quaker Mary Tuke, who opened a grocery shop in 1725. It was eventually inherited by the Rowntree family, who took their responsibilities to the poor very seriously indeed. As well as establishing the famous chocolate factory which brought considerable employment, their charitable achievements included the founding of a model village by Joseph Rowntree to house their workers (all amenities were included except, of course, a public house!) His son B.S. (Seebohm) Rowntree wrote 'Poverty: a Study of Town Life', which did much to highlight the conditions of the industrialised working class.*

MERCHANT ADVENTURERS' HALL, YORK

This magnificent beamed interior has been lovingly preserved, and today is still almost exactly as the Merchant Adventurers themselves would have seen it.

PINEAPPLE AND KIRSCH CREAM FLAN   *Serves 4*

In this easy-to-make party piece topped with golden nuts, a chocolatey base with a crunchy texture complements the fresh but creamy filling.

Metric		*lb/oz*	*U.S.A.*
80 g	*Butter*	3 oz	5 tbsp
25 g	*Plain chocolate*	1 oz	1 square
375 g	*Plain chocolate digestive biscuits*	12 oz	12 oz
300 ml	*Double cream*	½ pt	1 cup
2 tbsp	*Kirsch*	2 tbsp	3 tbsp
125 g	*Caster sugar*	4 oz	½ cup
500 g	*Pineapple, canned*	1 lb	1 lb
30 g	*Almonds, chopped*	1 oz	¼ cup

1. Place the butter and chocolate in a basin over a pan of hot water, stirring occasionally until melted.
2. Put the biscuits into a polythene bag and crush with a rolling pin. Add the crumbs to the butter and chocolate. Mix together well.
3. Press the biscuit mixture into a well-greased 20 cm (8") flan tin with a loose bottom. Place in the refrigerator for about 30 minutes to set.
4. Put the cream into a bowl and whip until thick. Add the kirsch and the sugar.
5. Drain and chop the pineapple and stir into the cream. Pour the mixture into the biscuit base and place in the refrigerator to chill.
6. Put the almonds on to a baking tray and roast in a hot oven for a few minutes until golden brown. Allow to cool and sprinkle over the pineapple cream.

REDCURRANT AND ALMOND BAKE   *Serves 4*

Redcurrants are only in season for a short while, so make a note of this super recipe when they are around. Warmed, tinned peach slices can be substituted for a lovely winter pudding.

Metric		lb/oz	U.S.A.
250 g	Shortcrust pastry	8 oz	8 oz
2 tbsp	Apricot jam	2 tbsp	3 tbsp
125 g	Unsalted butter	4 oz	½ cup
125 g	Caster sugar	4 oz	½ cup
2	Eggs	2	2
125 g	Ground almonds	4 oz	1 cup
500 g	Redcurrants	1 lb	1 lb
150 ml	Cream	¼ pt	½ cup

1. Roll out the pastry and line a deep 20 cm (8") flan tin. Prick the bottom with a fork.
2. Melt the apricot jam gently in a small saucepan then brush over the bottom of the pastry.
3. Soften the butter then beat in the sugar and eggs until the mixture is light and fluffy. Stir in the ground almonds. Pour the almond mixture into the flan tin.
4. Place in a moderate oven, 190°C, 375°F, Gas Mark 5, for 35 minutes until golden brown.
5. Put the redcurrants into a saucepan with 1 tablespoon of water and gently simmer until the fruit is tender. Drain the liquid off and place the fruit on top of the pudding.
6. Serve hot with whipped cream.

BLACKBERRY AND WALNUT FLAN

Serves 10

Wild blackberries can still be found in
Yorkshire's hedgerows. If you've the
time to go out and pick them they will
add a special 'perfumed' flavour to this
flan.

Metric		lb/oz	U.S.A.
350 g	Flour	12 oz	3 cups
75 g	Walnuts	3 oz	¾ cup
1 tsp	Cinnamon	1 tsp	1 tsp
175 g	Icing sugar	6 oz	¾ cup
175 g	Butter	6 oz	¾ cup
2	Eggs, beaten	2	2
500 g	Blackberries	1 lb	1 lb
2 tbsp	Caster sugar	2 tbsp	3 tbsp
250 g	Blackcurrant jam	8 oz	8 oz
1	Lemon, juice of	1	1
300 ml	Double cream	½ pt	1 cup

1. Put the flour with a pinch of salt into a bowl. Place the
   walnuts in a liquidiser and grind finely. Add to the flour
   with the cinnamon and icing sugar.
2. Rub in the butter. Mix to a stiff dough with the beaten
   eggs and a little cold water if necessary.
3. Knead the pastry until it is smooth, then wrap and chill for
   at least 1 hour.
4. Roll out the pastry and line a 30 cm (12") flan tin. Bake
   the pastry blind: prick the bottom of the flan with a fork,
   then cover with greaseproof paper. Fill with rice or beans.
   Place in a hot oven, 200°C, 400°F, Gas Mark 6, for 10
   minutes then reduce the heat to 180°C, 350°F, Gas Mark
   4 for a further 20 minutes.
5. When the pastry is cooked, remove from the oven and
   remove the beans and greaseproof. Replace the flan in the
   oven for just a few minutes to dry the bottom. Remove
   from the oven and allow to cool.
6. Wash the blackberries and place in a pan with 1
   tablespoon of water and the caster sugar. Bring gently to
   the boil and simmer for a few minutes.
7. Remove the blackberries with a strainer spoon and allow
   to cool.
8. Add the blackcurrant jam to the blackberry juice in the
   saucepan and heat gently until the jam has melted. Add
   the lemon juice to the saucepan and allow to cool.
9. Brush a little glaze over the bottom of the flan. Arrange
   the blackberries in the flan case and pour over the rest of
   the glaze.
10. Place in the refrigerator to cool and serve with whipped
    cream.

CHEF H. BRAND'S LIQUEUR PARFAIT *Serves 6*

Hodgson's Restaurant have come up with all the ingredients for the perfect parfait — cream, sugar and . . . Grand Marnier!

Metric		lb/oz	U.S.A.
125 g	Caster sugar	4 oz	½ cup
4	Egg yolks, beaten	4	4
300 ml	Double cream	½ pt	1 cup
3 tbsp	Grand Marnier	3 tbsp	¼ cup
3	Egg whites	3	3

1. Place three-quarters of the sugar in a pan with 150 ml (¼ pt, ½ cup) of water and boil for 3–4 minutes until you have a heavy syrup. Remove from the heat.
2. Allow the syrup to cool a little then beat in the egg yolks until you have 'ribbons' of egg yolk in the syrup.
3. Whip the cream until stiff then stir in the liqueur.
4. Place the egg whites in a clean dry bowl and beat until stiff. Add the remaining sugar and beat again.
5. Mix the cream and syrup then fold in the egg whites. Spoon into a mould, e.g. a bread tin, and place in the freezer overnight.
6. One hour before serving, remove from the freezer and allow to soften in the refrigerator.

OLD ENGLISH SYLLABUB *Serves 6*

"For he on honey-dew hath fed,
And drunk the milk of Paradise." Kubla Khan
SAMUEL TAYLOR COLERIDGE, 1772-1834

A stunningly simple dessert from the Micklegate Restaurant. Light, lemony, and with a hint of sherry.

Metric		lb/oz	U.S.A.
1	Egg white	1	1
2 drops	Yellow food colouring	2 drops	2 drops
4 tbsp	Caster sugar	4 tbsp	⅓ cup
600 ml	Whipping cream	1 pt	2½ cups
5	Lemons	5	5
1	Sherry, measure	1	1

1. Whip the egg white until stiff. Put the yellow colouring into half of the sugar and stir well until yellow. Squeeze 4 lemons and slice one.
2. Dip the rim of a wine glass first into the egg white and then into the coloured sugar to frost the edge.
3. Place all the remaining ingredients except the lemon slices into a large bowl and whip until thick.
4. Spoon the mixture into the frosted glasses and decorate each one with a twisted slice of lemon.

GOOSEBERRY MERINGUE FLAN

Serves 6

Forget the diet! Don't miss out on this delectable dessert as served at St. William's Restaurant, York.

Metric		lb/oz	U.S.A.
200 g	Shortcrust pastry	7 oz	7 oz
450 g	Gooseberries, topped and tailed	1 lb	1 lb
275 g	Caster sugar	10 oz	1 ¼ cups
1 tbsp	Cornflour	1 tbsp	1 tbsp
½ tsp	Cinnamon	½ tsp	½ tsp
½ tsp	Nutmeg	½ tsp	½ tsp
2	Eggs, separated	2	2

1. Set the oven to 200°C, 400°F, Gas Mark 6.
2. Roll out the pastry on a floured board and line a 20 cm (8") flan case. Bake blind for 15 minutes until golden brown. Remove from the oven and reset the oven to 180°C, 350°F, Gas Mark 4.
3. Put the gooseberries into a pan with a little water and 175 g (6 oz, ¾ cup) of the sugar. Simmer gently until soft.
4. Mix the cornflour to a smooth paste with a little cold water, add to the fruit and boil until the juice begins to thicken slightly then stir in the cinnamon and nutmeg. Remove from the heat and allow to cool.
5. Beat the yolks into the mixture and pour into the flan.
6. Whisk the whites until stiff, add half the remaining sugar and whisk again. Fold in the rest of the sugar and spread over the fruit in the pastry case.
7. Place in the oven and cook for 10 minutes until the meringue is crisp and lightly brown.

TOFFEE SLICES

Serves 4

A great stand-by pudding or tea-time treat very popular with children of all ages!

Metric		lb/oz	U.S.A.
	4 Slices of bread		
150 ml	Milk	¼ pt	½ cup
50 g	Butter	2 oz	¼ cup
50 g	Granulated sugar	2 oz	4 tbsp
125 g	Golden syrup	4 oz	¼ cup

1. Cut each slice of bread in half. Place the milk in a basin and dip each piece of bread in it. Place the bread on a plate to drain.
2. Melt the butter, granulated sugar and golden syrup in a large pan and bring to the boil.
3. Fry the bread in the syrup mixture until each piece is golden. Serve immediately.

YORKSHIRE FRUIT LOAVES　　　　　　　　*Makes 3*

If you are a home-baked bread lover, try these delicious rich fruit loaves from Woodhead's Bakery. When spread generously with butter, irresistible is putting it mildly!

Metric		lb/oz	U.S.A.
325 g	Strong white flour	12 oz	3 cups
50 g	Caster sugar	1½ oz	¼ cup
40 g	Butter	1¼ oz	¼ cup
15 g	Fresh yeast	½ oz	1 tbsp
2 drops	Yellow food colouring	2 drops	2 drops
50 g	Currants	1½ oz	⅓ cup
50 g	Sultanas	1½ oz	⅓ cup
25 g	Mixed peel	¾ oz	1 tbsp
50 g	Butter, melted	1½ oz	¼ cup
50 g	Granulated sugar	1½ oz	¼ cup

1. Sift the flour, a pinch of salt and the caster sugar on to a work top and gently rub in the butter until the mixture resembles breadcrumbs. Make a circle and place the yeast in the centre. (You may use a bowl if you find it easier than the work surface!)
2. Add the food colouring to 150 ml (¼ pt, ½ cup) warm water. Then pour over the yeast to dissolve. Add the remaining water to the flour gradually and mix to a soft dough adding a little more water if needed and kneading until smooth. Cover with a damp cloth and leave in a warm place to ferment for 45 minutes.
3. Set the oven to 200°C, 400°F, Gas Mark 6. Grease three bread tins. Wash the fruit in warm water and dry in a clean cloth.
4. When the dough is well risen, mix in the fruit, cover again and leave for a further 15 minutes.
5. Divide into three, mould into rounds and leave to rest for 2 minutes. Mould into final shapes and place in the tins. Cover with a clean cloth and leave in a warm place for approximately 35 minutes to rise.
6. Bake for 20–25 minutes. When cooked remove from the tin, brush the top with the melted butter and sprinkle immediately with granulated sugar.

A YORKSHIREMAN'S ADVICE TO HIS SON

"See all, hear all, say nowt,
Eat all, sup all, pay nowt,
And if tha does owt for nowt,
Allus do it for thisen!"

YORKSHIRE PARKIN

Fresh batches of these two traditional recipes are baked daily at Woodhead's Bakery. They are popular not only with visitors eager to sample Yorkshire fare, but also with regular customers. Scrumptious tea-time treats are a *must* in every Yorkshire home!

Metric		lb/oz	U.S.A.
425 g	*White flour, sifted*	14 oz	3½ cups
230 g	*Sugar*	8 oz	1 cup
15 g	*Malt extract*	½ oz	½ oz
450 g	*Medium oatmeal*	1 lb	4 cups
12 g	*Ground ginger*	2 tsp	2 tsp
12 g	*Bicarbonate of soda*	2 tsp	2 tsp
230 g	*White fat*	8 oz	1 cup
480 g	*Golden syrup*	1 lb	1½ cups

1. Grease a roasting tin 25 cm (10") square. Set the oven to 180°C, 350°F, Gas Mark 4.
2. Mix all the dry ingredients together. Add the fat and rub into the mixture.
3. Heat the golden syrup, add 400 ml (⅔ pt, 1¼ cups) of hot water, and combine together.
4. Pour into the dry ingredients, mix together and beat for 2 minutes. Pour into the prepared tin and level the top.
5. Bake for about 25 minutes, until a skewer comes out clean when inserted in the centre. Allow to cool in the tin, then cut into squares.

PARKIN is a type of gingerbread, the distinctive ingredient being oatmeal. Its origins go back to pagan times, and it is traditionally eaten in the North of England in autumn, being particularly associated with All Hallow's Eve (Halloween) on 31st October, All Saints' Day (1st November) and — more latterly — Guy Fawkes' night on the fifth of November.

IN HIGH PETERGATE—*where Guy's parents lived and he was probably born — the celebration of his demise is regarded as somewhat inappropriate. St Peter's School, where Guy was a pupil, loyally refuses to join the rest of the country in its celebrations on the grounds that it would be bad form to burn an old boy!*

HOLY TRINITY IN MICKLEGATE *has a memorial to* **Dr. John Burton** *the historian who is said to have been the original of* **Dr. Slop** *in Sterne's* **Tristram Shandy**. *Sterne often came to York and was living outside York near Coxwood when he began writing this famous early novel. His opinion of the area seems to have been reflected through his stomach since he remarked — 'tis a land of plenty. I sit down alone to venison, fish and wild fowl, or a couple of fowls or ducks; with curds strawberries and cream'.*

YORKSHIRE CURD TART

Metric		lb/oz	U.S.A.
225 g	*Rich shortcrust pastry (see p. 74)*	8 oz	8 oz
	For the Yorkshire curd:		
125 g	*Butter*	4 oz	½ cup
125 g	*Sugar*	4 oz	½ cup
1 ½	*Eggs, beaten*	1 ½	1 ½
1	*Nutmeg, pinch of*	1	1
125 g	*Currants*	4 oz	⅔ cup
400 g	*Fresh curd cheese*	14 oz	1 ⅓ cups

1. Set the oven to 190°C, 375°F, Gas Mark 5.
2. Roll out the pastry to line a 15 cm (6") greased flan ring on a baking sheet or 12 tartlet tins. Using your thumb, make a fluted edge around the top of the ring. Refrigerate.
3. Place the butter and sugar in a bowl and beat until light. Using the eggs at room temperature, blend them into the fat and sugar in three equal amounts, beating well between each addition.
4. Stir the nutmeg and currants into the curd gently until well mixed.
5. Mix the butter and sugar into the curd mixture very gently. Fill the flan ring almost to the top and bake for about 35 minutes. Serve cold.

"Little Miss Muffet
Sat on a tuffet,
Eating her curds and whey;
There came a big spider,
Who sat down beside her
And frightened Miss Muffet away."

A HOST OF GOLDEN DAFFODILS!

Springtime visitors arriving by train are greeted by a magnificent display of daffodils along the wall as they walk towards York Minster.

ECCLES CAKES
Makes 12

Golden brown, melt-in-the-mouth currant cakes from the Theatre Royal Restaurant, York. Perfect for afternoon tea, or whenever you so desire!

Metric		*lb/oz*	*U.S.A.*
450 g	*Puff pastry*	1 lb	1 lb
125 g	*Butter, softened*	4 oz	½ cup
250 g	*Currants**	8 oz	1⅓ cups
125 g	*Demerara sugar*	4 oz	¾ cup

* Chopped peel and a little cinnamon may be added with the currants, if liked.

1. Set the oven to 210°C, 425°F, Gas Mark 7.
2. Roll out the pastry on a floured board and cut into twelve 6 cm (2½") squares.
3. Place the butter, currants and sugar in a bowl, and mix well.
4. Spoon equal amounts of mixture into the centre of each square, then dampen the edges with a little water.

5. Gather and pinch the edges together, turn upside down (with pinched edges on the floured board) and roll gently into a circular 'bun' with the currants just visible under the pastry.
6. Brush with water and sprinkle with a little sugar. Make two or three slits in each top.
7. Place on a greased baking tray and bake for 10–15 minutes until golden brown.

THE CITY WALL

A three mile stroll along the City Wall will take you around York's medieval boundaries. The substantial dimensions — it is 13' high and 6' wide — were designed to protect the inhabitants. Nowadays they provide a fascinating tour route of the city limits in the Middle Ages, with superb views of the ancient and picturesque buildings.

The gap in the wall between Hayerbridge and the Red Tower was originally marshland and so sufficient in itself to prevent people from trying to enter the city illegally!

SICILIAN SLICE

Makes 9 squares

This light pastry case with a delicious almond filling is another speciality from Woodhead's Bakery.

Metric		lb/oz	U.S.A.
	For the rich shortcrust pastry:		
250 g	Flour	8 oz	2 cups
150 g	Butter	5 oz	½ cup
1	Egg, beaten	1	1
50 g	Sugar	2 oz	¼ cup
	For the filling:		
150 g	Sugar	4 oz	½ cup
75 g	Ground almonds	2 oz	½ cup
150 g	Butter	4 oz	⅔ cup
2	Eggs, beaten	2	2
75 g	Flour, sifted	2 oz	½ cup
140 g	Mixed peel	3 oz	⅓ cup
3 tbsp	Apricot jam	3 tbsp	¼ cup
30 g	Flaked hazelnuts (or almonds)	1 oz	¼ cup

1. Set the oven to 190°C, 375°F, Gas Mark 5.
2. Sift the flour into a bowl with a pinch of salt. Gently rub in the butter until the mixture resembles breadcrumbs.
3. Mix the egg and sugar together then add to the flour. Mix to a dough (do not overmix) and refrigerate for 30 minutes.
4. To make the filling, place the sugar, ground almonds and butter in a bowl and beat until light. Blend in the eggs a little at a time. When well mixed, fold in the flour and peel.
5. Roll out the pastry and line the base of a greased 23 cm (9") square tin.
6. Spread a thin layer of apricot jam on the pastry. Place the ground almond mixture on top of the jam and spread carefully to level it. Sprinkle lightly with flaked hazelnuts.
7. Bake for 30 minutes and cut into squares when cold.

WAS ROBIN HOOD A YORKSHIREMAN? *Everyone has heard of Sicilian bandits, but the most famous 'bandit' of all time was surely Robin Hood. Revered as a friend of the poor, some people make a very good case for the argument that he was a Yorkshireman! Take, for example, the number of inns and areas that incorporate 'Robin Hood' in their names. At Robin Hood's Bay on the east coast, the famous outlaw is said to have kept fishing vessels hidden in order to make his escape should the sheriff's men come too close. There is also a gravestone in the grounds of a ruined nunnery at Kirklees, near Brighouse, that bears an inscription stating that Robin Hood, Earl of Huntingdon lies there.*

SAUCES   These relate to recipes earlier in the book.

Many sauces and gravies are now packaged
to help the busy cook save time, but the
home-made variety is always special. The
tomato and brown sauce freeze well — it
saves time to make a larger quantity and
freeze it in portions.

Demi-glace and Espagnole sauces
If you don't have time to make these basic brown sauces, a
good, well thickened gravy may be substituted. Don't forget to
add some sherry for a demi-glace!

Demi-glace sauce
To make a demi-glace sauce, put equal quantities of Espagnole
sauce (below) and strong beef stock into a heavy pan (with a
few mushrooms). Simmer until the sauce is reduced by at
least half. Remove, strain and re-heat. Remove from the heat
and stir in a little dry sherry.

Espagnole sauce   *Makes approx. 450 ml (¾ pt, 1 ½ cups)*

Metric		lb/oz	U.S.A.
25 g	Ham or bacon (raw), chopped	1 tbsp	1 tbsp
30 g	Butter	1 oz	1 tbsp
1	Carrot, peeled and chopped	1	1
1	Onion, chopped	1	1
3 tbsp	Mushroom stalks, chopped	3 tbsp	⅓ cup
2 tbsp	Celery, chopped (optional)	2 tbsp	¼ cup
1	Beef stock cube	1	1
45 g	Flour	1 ½ oz	¼ cup
2 tbsp	Tomato paste	2 tbsp	¼ cup
250 g	Tomatoes, peeled and chopped	8 oz	2 cups
1 tsp	Thyme	1 tsp	1 tsp
1	Bay leaf	1	1

1. Cook the bacon in the butter for a few minutes.
2. Add the vegetables and sauté gently for 5–8 minutes.
3. Make a stock with the cube and 300 ml (½ pt, 1 cup)
   boiling water. Set aside.
4. Stir the flour into the vegetable mixture. Continue stirring
   until the flour browns well, then add the stock very
   gradually, stirring continuously.
5. When the sauce has thickened, stir in the tomato paste,
   tomatoes, thyme and bay leaf. Season lightly.
6. Simmer for 30 minutes, stirring occasionally and skimming
   off excess fat. Taste and correct the seasoning.
7. Strain the sauce into a basin and cover the surface with
   damp greaseproof or clingwrap to stop a skin forming.

Noilly cream sauce

Bring 125 ml (¼ pt, ½ cup) of double cream to the boil. When it thickens stir in the same amount of Noilly Prat and bring back to the boil.

Port and mushroom cream sauce

Cook 250 g (8 oz, 2 cups) of sliced mushrooms in a little butter. Add 90 ml (3½ fl. oz, ⅜ cup) of port and bring to the boil. Remove from the heat and stir in 125 ml (4 fl. oz, ½ cup) of double cream. Cook until the sauce thickens.

Béchamel sauce
Makes approx. 300 ml (½ pt, 1 cup)

Metric		lb/oz	U.S.A.
300 ml	Milk	½ pt	1 cup
1	Small onion, chopped	1	⅓ cup
1	Carrot, chopped	1	1
1	Stick of celery, chopped	1	1
1	Bay leaf	1	1
1	Clove	1	1
½ tsp	Mace, ground	½ tsp	½ tsp
2	Peppercorns	2	2
30 g	Butter	1 oz	2 tbsp
45 g	Flour	1½ oz	¼ cup

1. Place the milk and vegetables in a saucepan and bring slowly to the boil, then add the herbs and spices. Cover the pan with a tightly fitting lid.
2. Remove the saucepan from the heat and leave covered for half an hour to infuse.
3. Strain off the milk and remove the vegetables from the pan.
4. Melt the butter in the pan slowly, add the flour and cook for a few minutes, stirring all the time. Be careful not to brown the mixture.
5. Stir the flavoured milk gradually into the flour until the mixture is smooth. Then bring to the boil and simmer for 2–3 minutes, stirring all the time.

Clarified butter

To clarify butter, melt over a gentle heat. Remove and set aside until the milky solids settle. Skim the clarified butter from the top and transfer to a covered bowl. Refrigerate until needed.

MARSDEN, NEW ZEALAND *The Reverend Samuel Marsden, who was one of the first missionaries to go to New Zealand, originally hailed from Yorkshire. He was the son of a Yorkshire blacksmith and was trained by an evangelical society there before setting off for the Southern hemisphere.*

Index

Continued overleaf

78

RESTAURANTS & HOTELS

We would like to thank the following for their help and generosity in giving us the recipes listed below. Local telephone numbers are also provided.

EMILIO'S RESTAURANT, 3 Ripon Road, Harrogate   65267
Proprietor/chef: Emilio Rivera
Calamares en su Tinta, 17
Paella de mariscos, 44
Luncheon: 12-2.15 pm. Dinner: 7-11 pm (Mon-Sat)

HODGSON'S RESTAURANT,   509866
RUSSELL HOTEL, Valley Drive, Harrogate
Manager: Martin Hodgson
Chef: Richard Hodgson
Trout snuggles, 15
Mousseline of turkey with song thrush sauce, 42
Lobster princess, 60
Salmon with Champagne sauce, 52
Chef H. Brand's liqueur parfait, 67
Dinner: 7.30-10.30 pm (Tues-Sat)

HOSPITALITY INN,   64601
West Park, Prospect Place, Harrogate
Chef: Nigel Mason
Deep fried mushrooms with cucumber mayonnaise, 11
Rack of English lamb with honey and mint, 30
Loin of pork Victoria, 31
Whole lemon sole stuffed with crabmeat, 59
Luncheon: 12-2 pm. Dinner: 7-9.30 pm (7 days)

HOTEL MAJESTIC, Ripon Road, Harrogate   68972
Chef: David Kirkpatrick
Leg of lamb cooked in pastry, 30
Tipsy duck with veal and pepper stuffing, 42
Gruyère and shellfish soufflé, 54
Luncheon: 12.45-1.45 pm (Mon-Fri)
Dinner: 6.45-9.15 pm (7 days)

MICKLEGATE RESTAURANT,   58301
THE LADBROKE ABBEY PARK HOTEL, The Mount, York
Chef: Paul Woollons
   Yorkshire pudding, 22
   Old English syllabub, 67
Dinner: 6.30-9.30 pm. (7 days)

NUMBER 6 RESTAURANT, 6 Ripon Road, Harrogate   502908
Chef: J. Beardsley
   Hot creamed Morecambe shrimps, 14
   Escalopes de veau Savoyarde, 34
   Poussin rôti au Champagne, 39
Dinner: 7.30-10 pm (closed Mondays)

RISTORANTE BARI, The Shambles, York   33807
Proprietors: Paul and Carol Collins
Chefs: Angelo, Mario and Franco
   Avocado Mediterrano, 12
   Filletto Casanova, 25
   Bistecca alla pizzaiola, 28
   Saltimbocca, 34
   Canestrella alla crema, 50
   Spaghetti alla vongole, 53
Luncheon: 11.30 am-2.30 pm. Dinner: 6-11 pm (7 days)

THEATRE ROYAL RESTAURANT, Theatre Royal,   32596
St. Leonard's Place, York
Manageress: Helen Sykes
Cooks: Susan Swindell and Joanna Garbutt
   Cucumber and grapefruit salad, 14
   Cucumber and pineapple salad, 14
   Curried rice salad, 14
   Steak and kidney pudding, 26
   Eccles cakes, 72
Luncheon: 12.30-2 pm. Dinner: 7-9.30 pm (Mon-Sat)

ST. WILLIAM'S RESTAURANT, 2 College Street, York   34830
Manageress: Sue Hepton
   Smoked haddock mousse, 52
   Gooseberry meringue flan, 68
Open: 10 am-5 pm (Mon-Sat)

THE VIKING HOTEL, North Street, York   59822
Chef: Stuart Wynne
   Paupiettes de boeuf, 27
   Double crust chicken pie, 36
   Chicken calypso, 38
Open: Carvery: 12.30-2 pm and 7-10 pm (7 days)
Restaurant: 7-10 pm (Mon-Thurs). 6.30-10 pm (Fri & Sat)
Plume's Steak bar: 7-11 pm (Tues-Sat)

WOODHEAD'S BAKERY, 13 Saint Sampson's Square, York   52767
Proprietors: Messrs Woodhead (Scarborough) Ltd.
   Yorkshire fruit loaves, 69
   Yorkshire parkin, 70
   Yorkshire curd tart, 71
   Sicilian slice, 74
Open: 8.45 am-5 pm (Mon-Sat)

MEASURES & CONVERSIONS

Please read the notes on measures and conversions on page 4. The table below will help our American readers.

English	American
Bicarbonate of soda	Baking soda
Caster sugar	Fine granulated sugar
Cornflour	Cornstarch
Demerara sugar	Soft light brown sugar
Digestive biscuits	Graham crackers
Dripping	White fat
Double cream	Heavy cream
Flaked almonds	Slivered almonds
Glacé cherries	Candied red cherries
Golden syrup	Light corn syrup
Grill	Broil
Lard	White fat
Plain chocolate	Semi-sweet chocolate
Redcurrant jelly	Cranberry jelly
Single cream	Light cream
Streaky bacon rashers	Canadian bacon strips
Sultanas	Light raisins

Farewell

Not being forthright Yorkshire folk, nor having any connection with their dashing hero, Dick Turpin, we are not quite brave enough to demand STAND AND DELIVER! YOUR MONEY OR YOUR LIFE! But we hope you have enjoyed this book enough to seek out others in the series whilst on your travels. Current titles are listed below.

Titles available now:

Bath
Cambridge
Edinburgh
The Heart of the Cotswolds
Oxford
Stratford-upon-Avon
York and Harrogate

In preparation:

Brighton
Cheltenham and Gloucester
Hampstead and Highgate
Kensington and Chelsea
Soho
Windsor and Hampton Court